T0355260

International Relations: A Very Short Introduction

VERY SHORT INTRODUCTIONS are for anyone wanting a stimulating and accessible way into a new subject. They are written by experts, and have been translated into more than 45 different languages.

The series began in 1995, and now covers a wide variety of topics in every discipline. The VSI library currently contains over 650 volumes—a *Very Short Introduction* to everything from Psychology and Philosophy of Science to American History and Relativity—and continues to grow in every subject area.

Very Short Introductions available now:

ABOLITIONISM Richard S. Newman
THE ABRAHAMIC RELIGIONS
    Charles L. Cohen
ACCOUNTING Christopher Nobes
ADAM SMITH Christopher J. Berry
ADOLESCENCE Peter K. Smith
ADVERTISING Winston Fletcher
AERIAL WARFARE Frank Ledwidge
AESTHETICS Bence Nanay
AFRICAN AMERICAN RELIGION
    Eddie S. Glaude Jr
AFRICAN HISTORY John Parker and
    Richard Rathbone
AFRICAN POLITICS Ian Taylor
AFRICAN RELIGIONS
    Jacob K. Olupona
AGEING Nancy A. Pachana
AGNOSTICISM Robin Le Poidevin
AGRICULTURE Paul Brassley and
    Richard Soffe
ALBERT CAMUS Oliver Gloag
ALEXANDER THE GREAT
    Hugh Bowden
ALGEBRA Peter M. Higgins
AMERICAN CULTURAL HISTORY
    Eric Avila
AMERICAN FOREIGN RELATIONS
    Andrew Preston
AMERICAN HISTORY Paul S. Boyer
AMERICAN IMMIGRATION
    David A. Gerber
AMERICAN LEGAL HISTORY
    G. Edward White
AMERICAN NAVAL HISTORY
    Craig L. Symonds

AMERICAN POLITICAL HISTORY
    Donald Critchlow
AMERICAN POLITICAL PARTIES
    AND ELECTIONS L. Sandy Maisel
AMERICAN POLITICS
    Richard M. Valelly
THE AMERICAN PRESIDENCY
    Charles O. Jones
THE AMERICAN REVOLUTION
    Robert J. Allison
AMERICAN SLAVERY
    Heather Andrea Williams
THE AMERICAN WEST Stephen Aron
AMERICAN WOMEN'S HISTORY
    Susan Ware
ANAESTHESIA Aidan O'Donnell
ANALYTIC PHILOSOPHY
    Michael Beaney
ANARCHISM Colin Ward
ANCIENT ASSYRIA Karen Radner
ANCIENT EGYPT Ian Shaw
ANCIENT EGYPTIAN ART AND
    ARCHITECTURE Christina Riggs
ANCIENT GREECE Paul Cartledge
THE ANCIENT NEAR EAST
    Amanda H. Podany
ANCIENT PHILOSOPHY Julia Annas
ANCIENT WARFARE
    Harry Sidebottom
ANGELS David Albert Jones
ANGLICANISM Mark Chapman
THE ANGLO-SAXON AGE
    John Blair
ANIMAL BEHAVIOUR
    Tristram D. Wyatt

THE ANIMAL KINGDOM
    Peter Holland
ANIMAL RIGHTS David DeGrazia
THE ANTARCTIC Klaus Dodds
ANTHROPOCENE Erle C. Ellis
ANTISEMITISM Steven Beller
ANXIETY Daniel Freeman and
    Jason Freeman
THE APOCRYPHAL GOSPELS
    Paul Foster
APPLIED MATHEMATICS
    Alain Goriely
ARCHAEOLOGY Paul Bahn
ARCHITECTURE Andrew Ballantyne
ARISTOCRACY William Doyle
ARISTOTLE Jonathan Barnes
ART HISTORY Dana Arnold
ART THEORY Cynthia Freeland
ARTIFICIAL INTELLIGENCE
    Margaret A. Boden
ASIAN AMERICAN HISTORY
    Madeline Y. Hsu
ASTROBIOLOGY David C. Catling
ASTROPHYSICS James Binney
ATHEISM Julian Baggini
THE ATMOSPHERE Paul I. Palmer
AUGUSTINE Henry Chadwick
AUSTRALIA Kenneth Morgan
AUTISM Uta Frith
AUTOBIOGRAPHY Laura Marcus
THE AVANT GARDE David Cottington
THE AZTECS Davíd Carrasco
BABYLONIA Trevor Bryce
BACTERIA Sebastian G. B. Amyes
BANKING John Goddard and
    John O. S. Wilson
BARTHES Jonathan Culler
THE BEATS David Sterritt
BEAUTY Roger Scruton
BEHAVIOURAL ECONOMICS
    Michelle Baddeley
BESTSELLERS John Sutherland
THE BIBLE John Riches
BIBLICAL ARCHAEOLOGY
    Eric H. Cline
BIG DATA Dawn E. Holmes
BIOGRAPHY Hermione Lee
BIOMETRICS Michael Fairhurst
BLACK HOLES Katherine Blundell
BLOOD Chris Cooper
THE BLUES Elijah Wald

THE BODY Chris Shilling
THE BOOK OF COMMON PRAYER
    Brian Cummings
THE BOOK OF MORMON
    Terryl Givens
BORDERS Alexander C. Diener and
    Joshua Hagen
THE BRAIN Michael O'Shea
BRANDING Robert Jones
THE BRICS Andrew F. Cooper
THE BRITISH CONSTITUTION
    Martin Loughlin
THE BRITISH EMPIRE Ashley Jackson
BRITISH POLITICS Anthony Wright
BUDDHA Michael Carrithers
BUDDHISM Damien Keown
BUDDHIST ETHICS Damien Keown
BYZANTIUM Peter Sarris
C. S. LEWIS James Como
CALVINISM Jon Balserak
CANCER Nicholas James
CAPITALISM James Fulcher
CATHOLICISM Gerald O'Collins
CAUSATION Stephen Mumford and
    Rani Lill Anjum
THE CELL Terence Allen and
    Graham Cowling
THE CELTS Barry Cunliffe
CHAOS Leonard Smith
CHARLES DICKENS Jenny Hartley
CHEMISTRY Peter Atkins
CHILD PSYCHOLOGY Usha Goswami
CHILDREN'S LITERATURE
    Kimberley Reynolds
CHINESE LITERATURE Sabina Knight
CHOICE THEORY Michael Allingham
CHRISTIAN ART Beth Williamson
CHRISTIAN ETHICS D. Stephen Long
CHRISTIANITY Linda Woodhead
CIRCADIAN RHYTHMS
    Russell Foster and Leon Kreitzman
CITIZENSHIP Richard Bellamy
CIVIL ENGINEERING
    David Muir Wood
CLASSICAL LITERATURE William Allan
CLASSICAL MYTHOLOGY
    Helen Morales
CLASSICS Mary Beard and
    John Henderson
CLAUSEWITZ Michael Howard
CLIMATE Mark Maslin

CLIMATE CHANGE Mark Maslin
CLINICAL PSYCHOLOGY
    Susan Llewelyn and
    Katie Aafjes-van Doorn
COGNITIVE NEUROSCIENCE
    Richard Passingham
THE COLD WAR Robert McMahon
COLONIAL AMERICA Alan Taylor
COLONIAL LATIN AMERICAN
    LITERATURE Rolena Adorno
COMBINATORICS Robin Wilson
COMEDY Matthew Bevis
COMMUNISM Leslie Holmes
COMPARATIVE LITERATURE
    Ben Hutchinson
COMPLEXITY John H. Holland
THE COMPUTER Darrel Ince
COMPUTER SCIENCE
    Subrata Dasgupta
CONCENTRATION CAMPS Dan Stone
CONFUCIANISM Daniel K. Gardner
THE CONQUISTADORS
    Matthew Restall and
    Felipe Fernández-Armesto
CONSCIENCE Paul Strohm
CONSCIOUSNESS Susan Blackmore
CONTEMPORARY ART
    Julian Stallabrass
CONTEMPORARY FICTION
    Robert Eaglestone
CONTINENTAL PHILOSOPHY
    Simon Critchley
COPERNICUS Owen Gingerich
CORAL REEFS Charles Sheppard
CORPORATE SOCIAL
    RESPONSIBILITY Jeremy Moon
CORRUPTION Leslie Holmes
COSMOLOGY Peter Coles
COUNTRY MUSIC Richard Carlin
CRIME FICTION Richard Bradford
CRIMINAL JUSTICE Julian V. Roberts
CRIMINOLOGY Tim Newburn
CRITICAL THEORY
    Stephen Eric Bronner
THE CRUSADES Christopher Tyerman
CRYPTOGRAPHY Fred Piper and
    Sean Murphy
CRYSTALLOGRAPHY A. M. Glazer
THE CULTURAL REVOLUTION
    Richard Curt Kraus
DADA AND SURREALISM
    David Hopkins
DANTE Peter Hainsworth and
    David Robey
DARWIN Jonathan Howard
THE DEAD SEA SCROLLS
    Timothy H. Lim
DECADENCE David Weir
DECOLONIZATION Dane Kennedy
DEMOCRACY Bernard Crick
DEMOGRAPHY Sarah Harper
DEPRESSION Jan Scott and
    Mary Jane Tacchi
DERRIDA Simon Glendinning
DESCARTES Tom Sorell
DESERTS Nick Middleton
DESIGN John Heskett
DEVELOPMENT Ian Goldin
DEVELOPMENTAL BIOLOGY
    Lewis Wolpert
THE DEVIL Darren Oldridge
DIASPORA Kevin Kenny
DICTIONARIES Lynda Mugglestone
DINOSAURS David Norman
DIPLOMACY Joseph M. Siracusa
DOCUMENTARY FILM
    Patricia Aufderheide
DREAMING J. Allan Hobson
DRUGS Les Iversen
DRUIDS Barry Cunliffe
DYNASTY Jeroen Duindam
DYSLEXIA Margaret J. Snowling
EARLY MUSIC Thomas Forrest Kelly
THE EARTH Martin Redfern
EARTH SYSTEM SCIENCE Tim Lenton
ECONOMICS Partha Dasgupta
EDUCATION Gary Thomas
EGYPTIAN MYTH Geraldine Pinch
EIGHTEENTH-CENTURY BRITAIN
    Paul Langford
THE ELEMENTS Philip Ball
EMOTION Dylan Evans
EMPIRE Stephen Howe
ENERGY SYSTEMS Nick Jenkins
ENGELS Terrell Carver
ENGINEERING David Blockley
THE ENGLISH LANGUAGE
    Simon Horobin
ENGLISH LITERATURE
    Jonathan Bate

THE ENLIGHTENMENT
   John Robertson
ENTREPRENEURSHIP Paul Westhead
   and Mike Wright
ENVIRONMENTAL ECONOMICS
   Stephen Smith
ENVIRONMENTAL ETHICS
   Robin Attfield
ENVIRONMENTAL LAW
   Elizabeth Fisher
ENVIRONMENTAL POLITICS
   Andrew Dobson
EPICUREANISM Catherine Wilson
EPIDEMIOLOGY Rodolfo Saracci
ETHICS Simon Blackburn
ETHNOMUSICOLOGY Timothy Rice
THE ETRUSCANS Christopher Smith
EUGENICS Philippa Levine
THE EUROPEAN UNION
   Simon Usherwood and John Pinder
EUROPEAN UNION LAW
   Anthony Arnull
EVOLUTION Brian and
   Deborah Charlesworth
EXISTENTIALISM Thomas Flynn
EXPLORATION Stewart A. Weaver
EXTINCTION Paul B. Wignall
THE EYE Michael Land
FAIRY TALE Marina Warner
FAMILY LAW Jonathan Herring
FASCISM Kevin Passmore
FASHION Rebecca Arnold
FEDERALISM Mark J. Rozell and
   Clyde Wilcox
FEMINISM Margaret Walters
FILM Michael Wood
FILM MUSIC Kathryn Kalinak
FILM NOIR James Naremore
THE FIRST WORLD WAR
   Michael Howard
FOLK MUSIC Mark Slobin
FOOD John Krebs
FORENSIC PSYCHOLOGY
   David Canter
FORENSIC SCIENCE Jim Fraser
FORESTS Jaboury Ghazoul
FOSSILS Keith Thomson
FOUCAULT Gary Gutting
THE FOUNDING FATHERS
   R. B. Bernstein

FRACTALS Kenneth Falconer
FREE SPEECH Nigel Warburton
FREE WILL Thomas Pink
FREEMASONRY Andreas Önnerfors
FRENCH LITERATURE John D. Lyons
THE FRENCH REVOLUTION
   William Doyle
FREUD Anthony Storr
FUNDAMENTALISM Malise Ruthven
FUNGI Nicholas P. Money
THE FUTURE Jennifer M. Gidley
GALAXIES John Gribbin
GALILEO Stillman Drake
GAME THEORY Ken Binmore
GANDHI Bhikhu Parekh
GARDEN HISTORY Gordon Campbell
GENES Jonathan Slack
GENIUS Andrew Robinson
GENOMICS John Archibald
GEOFFREY CHAUCER David Wallace
GEOGRAPHY John Matthews and
   David Herbert
GEOLOGY Jan Zalasiewicz
GEOPHYSICS William Lowrie
GEOPOLITICS Klaus Dodds
GERMAN LITERATURE Nicholas Boyle
GERMAN PHILOSOPHY
   Andrew Bowie
GLACIATION David J. A. Evans
GLOBAL CATASTROPHES Bill McGuire
GLOBAL ECONOMIC HISTORY
   Robert C. Allen
GLOBALIZATION Manfred Steger
GOD John Bowker
GOETHE Ritchie Robertson
THE GOTHIC Nick Groom
GOVERNANCE Mark Bevir
GRAVITY Timothy Clifton
THE GREAT DEPRESSION AND
   THE NEW DEAL Eric Rauchway
HABERMAS James Gordon Finlayson
THE HABSBURG EMPIRE
   Martyn Rady
HAPPINESS Daniel M. Haybron
THE HARLEM RENAISSANCE
   Cheryl A. Wall
THE HEBREW BIBLE AS LITERATURE
   Tod Linafelt
HEGEL Peter Singer
HEIDEGGER Michael Inwood

THE HELLENISTIC AGE
  Peter Thonemann
HEREDITY John Waller
HERMENEUTICS Jens Zimmermann
HERODOTUS Jennifer T. Roberts
HIEROGLYPHS Penelope Wilson
HINDUISM Kim Knott
HISTORY John H. Arnold
THE HISTORY OF ASTRONOMY
  Michael Hoskin
THE HISTORY OF CHEMISTRY
  William H. Brock
THE HISTORY OF CHILDHOOD
  James Marten
THE HISTORY OF CINEMA
  Geoffrey Nowell-Smith
THE HISTORY OF LIFE
  Michael Benton
THE HISTORY OF MATHEMATICS
  Jacqueline Stedall
THE HISTORY OF MEDICINE
  William Bynum
THE HISTORY OF PHYSICS
  J. L. Heilbron
THE HISTORY OF TIME
  Leofranc Holford-Strevens
HIV AND AIDS Alan Whiteside
HOBBES Richard Tuck
HOLLYWOOD Peter Decherney
THE HOLY ROMAN EMPIRE
  Joachim Whaley
HOME Michael Allen Fox
HOMER Barbara Graziosi
HORMONES Martin Luck
HUMAN ANATOMY
  Leslie Klenerman
HUMAN EVOLUTION Bernard Wood
HUMAN RIGHTS Andrew Clapham
HUMANISM Stephen Law
HUME A. J. Ayer
HUMOUR Noël Carroll
THE ICE AGE Jamie Woodward
IDENTITY Florian Coulmas
IDEOLOGY Michael Freeden
THE IMMUNE SYSTEM
  Paul Klenerman
INDIAN CINEMA Ashish Rajadhyaksha
INDIAN PHILOSOPHY Sue Hamilton
THE INDUSTRIAL REVOLUTION
  Robert C. Allen
INFECTIOUS DISEASE Marta L. Wayne
  and Benjamin M. Bolker
INFINITY Ian Stewart
INFORMATION Luciano Floridi
INNOVATION Mark Dodgson and
  David Gann
INTELLECTUAL PROPERTY
  Siva Vaidhyanathan
INTELLIGENCE Ian J. Deary
INTERNATIONAL LAW
  Vaughan Lowe
INTERNATIONAL MIGRATION
  Khalid Koser
INTERNATIONAL RELATIONS
  Christian Reus-Smit
INTERNATIONAL SECURITY
  Christopher S. Browning
IRAN Ali M. Ansari
ISLAM Malise Ruthven
ISLAMIC HISTORY Adam Silverstein
ISOTOPES Rob Ellam
ITALIAN LITERATURE
  Peter Hainsworth and David Robey
JESUS Richard Bauckham
JEWISH HISTORY David N. Myers
JOURNALISM Ian Hargreaves
JUDAISM Norman Solomon
JUNG Anthony Stevens
KABBALAH Joseph Dan
KAFKA Ritchie Robertson
KANT Roger Scruton
KEYNES Robert Skidelsky
KIERKEGAARD Patrick Gardiner
KNOWLEDGE Jennifer Nagel
THE KORAN Michael Cook
KOREA Michael J. Seth
LAKES Warwick F. Vincent
LANDSCAPE ARCHITECTURE
  Ian H. Thompson
LANDSCAPES AND
  GEOMORPHOLOGY
  Andrew Goudie and Heather Viles
LANGUAGES Stephen R. Anderson
LATE ANTIQUITY Gillian Clark
LAW Raymond Wacks
THE LAWS OF THERMODYNAMICS
  Peter Atkins
LEADERSHIP Keith Grint
LEARNING Mark Haselgrove
LEIBNIZ Maria Rosa Antognazza

LEO TOLSTOY Liza Knapp
LIBERALISM Michael Freeden
LIGHT Ian Walmsley
LINCOLN Allen C. Guelzo
LINGUISTICS Peter Matthews
LITERARY THEORY Jonathan Culler
LOCKE John Dunn
LOGIC Graham Priest
LOVE Ronald de Sousa
MACHIAVELLI Quentin Skinner
MADNESS Andrew Scull
MAGIC Owen Davies
MAGNA CARTA Nicholas Vincent
MAGNETISM Stephen Blundell
MALTHUS Donald Winch
MAMMALS T. S. Kemp
MANAGEMENT John Hendry
MAO Delia Davin
MARINE BIOLOGY Philip V. Mladenov
THE MARQUIS DE SADE John Phillips
MARTIN LUTHER Scott H. Hendrix
MARTYRDOM Jolyon Mitchell
MARX Peter Singer
MATERIALS Christopher Hall
MATHEMATICAL FINANCE
    Mark H. A. Davis
MATHEMATICS Timothy Gowers
MATTER Geoff Cottrell
THE MEANING OF LIFE
    Terry Eagleton
MEASUREMENT David Hand
MEDICAL ETHICS Michael Dunn and
    Tony Hope
MEDICAL LAW Charles Foster
MEDIEVAL BRITAIN John Gillingham
    and Ralph A. Griffiths
MEDIEVAL LITERATURE
    Elaine Treharne
MEDIEVAL PHILOSOPHY
    John Marenbon
MEMORY Jonathan K. Foster
METAPHYSICS Stephen Mumford
METHODISM William J. Abraham
THE MEXICAN REVOLUTION
    Alan Knight
MICHAEL FARADAY
    Frank A. J. L. James
MICROBIOLOGY Nicholas P. Money
MICROECONOMICS Avinash Dixit
MICROSCOPY Terence Allen

THE MIDDLE AGES Miri Rubin
MILITARY JUSTICE Eugene R. Fidell
MILITARY STRATEGY
    Antulio J. Echevarria II
MINERALS David Vaughan
MIRACLES Yujin Nagasawa
MODERN ARCHITECTURE
    Adam Sharr
MODERN ART David Cottington
MODERN CHINA Rana Mitter
MODERN DRAMA
    Kirsten E. Shepherd-Barr
MODERN FRANCE
    Vanessa R. Schwartz
MODERN INDIA Craig Jeffrey
MODERN IRELAND Senia Pašeta
MODERN ITALY Anna Cento Bull
MODERN JAPAN
    Christopher Goto-Jones
MODERN LATIN AMERICAN
    LITERATURE
    Roberto González Echevarría
MODERN WAR Richard English
MODERNISM Christopher Butler
MOLECULAR BIOLOGY Aysha Divan
    and Janice A. Royds
MOLECULES Philip Ball
MONASTICISM Stephen J. Davis
THE MONGOLS Morris Rossabi
MOONS David A. Rothery
MORMONISM Richard Lyman Bushman
MOUNTAINS Martin F. Price
MUHAMMAD Jonathan A. C. Brown
MULTICULTURALISM Ali Rattansi
MULTILINGUALISM John C. Maher
MUSIC Nicholas Cook
MYTH Robert A. Segal
NAPOLEON David Bell
THE NAPOLEONIC WARS
    Mike Rapport
NATIONALISM Steven Grosby
NATIVE AMERICAN LITERATURE
    Sean Teuton
NAVIGATION Jim Bennett
NAZI GERMANY Jane Caplan
NELSON MANDELA Elleke Boehmer
NEOLIBERALISM Manfred Steger and
    Ravi Roy
NETWORKS Guido Caldarelli and
    Michele Catanzaro

THE NEW TESTAMENT
Luke Timothy Johnson
THE NEW TESTAMENT AS
LITERATURE Kyle Keefer
NEWTON Robert Iliffe
NIELS BOHR J. L. Heilbron
NIETZSCHE Michael Tanner
NINETEENTH-CENTURY BRITAIN
Christopher Harvie and
H. C. G. Matthew
THE NORMAN CONQUEST
George Garnett
NORTH AMERICAN INDIANS
Theda Perdue and Michael D. Green
NORTHERN IRELAND
Marc Mulholland
NOTHING Frank Close
NUCLEAR PHYSICS Frank Close
NUCLEAR POWER Maxwell Irvine
NUCLEAR WEAPONS
Joseph M. Siracusa
NUMBERS Peter M. Higgins
NUTRITION David A. Bender
OBJECTIVITY Stephen Gaukroger
OCEANS Dorrik Stow
THE OLD TESTAMENT
Michael D. Coogan
THE ORCHESTRA D. Kern Holoman
ORGANIC CHEMISTRY
Graham Patrick
ORGANIZATIONS Mary Jo Hatch
ORGANIZED CRIME
Georgios A. Antonopoulos and
Georgios Papanicolaou
ORTHODOX CHRISTIANITY
A. Edward Siecienski
PAGANISM Owen Davies
PAIN Rob Boddice
THE PALESTINIAN-ISRAELI
CONFLICT Martin Bunton
PANDEMICS Christian W. McMillen
PARTICLE PHYSICS Frank Close
PAUL E. P. Sanders
PEACE Oliver P. Richmond
PENTECOSTALISM William K. Kay
PERCEPTION Brian Rogers
THE PERIODIC TABLE Eric R. Scerri
PHILOSOPHY Edward Craig
PHILOSOPHY IN THE ISLAMIC
WORLD Peter Adamson
PHILOSOPHY OF BIOLOGY
Samir Okasha
PHILOSOPHY OF LAW
Raymond Wacks
PHILOSOPHY OF SCIENCE
Samir Okasha
PHILOSOPHY OF RELIGION
Tim Bayne
PHOTOGRAPHY Steve Edwards
PHYSICAL CHEMISTRY Peter Atkins
PHYSICS Sidney Perkowitz
PILGRIMAGE Ian Reader
PLAGUE Paul Slack
PLANETS David A. Rothery
PLANTS Timothy Walker
PLATE TECTONICS Peter Molnar
PLATO Julia Annas
POETRY Bernard O'Donoghue
POLITICAL PHILOSOPHY David Miller
POLITICS Kenneth Minogue
POPULISM Cas Mudde and
Cristóbal Rovira Kaltwasser
POSTCOLONIALISM Robert Young
POSTMODERNISM Christopher Butler
POSTSTRUCTURALISM
Catherine Belsey
POVERTY Philip N. Jefferson
PREHISTORY Chris Gosden
PRESOCRATIC PHILOSOPHY
Catherine Osborne
PRIVACY Raymond Wacks
PROBABILITY John Haigh
PROGRESSIVISM Walter Nugent
PROHIBITION W. J. Rorabaugh
PROJECTS Andrew Davies
PROTESTANTISM Mark A. Noll
PSYCHIATRY Tom Burns
PSYCHOANALYSIS Daniel Pick
PSYCHOLOGY Gillian Butler and
Freda McManus
PSYCHOLOGY OF MUSIC
Elizabeth Hellmuth Margulis
PSYCHOPATHY Essi Viding
PSYCHOTHERAPY Tom Burns and
Eva Burns-Lundgren
PUBLIC ADMINISTRATION
Stella Z. Theodoulou and Ravi K. Roy
PUBLIC HEALTH Virginia Berridge
PURITANISM Francis J. Bremer
THE QUAKERS Pink Dandelion

QUANTUM THEORY
    John Polkinghorne
RACISM Ali Rattansi
RADIOACTIVITY Claudio Tuniz
RASTAFARI Ennis B. Edmonds
READING Belinda Jack
THE REAGAN REVOLUTION Gil Troy
REALITY Jan Westerhoff
RECONSTRUCTION Allen C. Guelzo
THE REFORMATION Peter Marshall
RELATIVITY Russell Stannard
RELIGION IN AMERICA Timothy Beal
THE RENAISSANCE Jerry Brotton
RENAISSANCE ART
    Geraldine A. Johnson
RENEWABLE ENERGY Nick Jelley
REPTILES T. S. Kemp
REVOLUTIONS Jack A. Goldstone
RHETORIC Richard Toye
RISK Baruch Fischhoff and John Kadvany
RITUAL Barry Stephenson
RIVERS Nick Middleton
ROBOTICS Alan Winfield
ROCKS Jan Zalasiewicz
ROMAN BRITAIN Peter Salway
THE ROMAN EMPIRE
    Christopher Kelly
THE ROMAN REPUBLIC
    David M. Gwynn
ROMANTICISM Michael Ferber
ROUSSEAU Robert Wokler
RUSSELL A. C. Grayling
RUSSIAN HISTORY Geoffrey Hosking
RUSSIAN LITERATURE Catriona Kelly
THE RUSSIAN REVOLUTION
    S. A. Smith
SAINTS Simon Yarrow
SAVANNAS Peter A. Furley
SCEPTICISM Duncan Pritchard
SCHIZOPHRENIA Chris Frith and
    Eve Johnstone
SCHOPENHAUER
    Christopher Janaway
SCIENCE AND RELIGION
    Thomas Dixon
SCIENCE FICTION David Seed
THE SCIENTIFIC REVOLUTION
    Lawrence M. Principe
SCOTLAND Rab Houston
SECULARISM Andrew Copson

SEXUAL SELECTION Marlene Zuk and
    Leigh W. Simmons
SEXUALITY Véronique Mottier
SHAKESPEARE'S COMEDIES
    Bart van Es
SHAKESPEARE'S SONNETS AND
    POEMS Jonathan F. S. Post
SHAKESPEARE'S TRAGEDIES
    Stanley Wells
SIKHISM Eleanor Nesbitt
THE SILK ROAD James A. Millward
SLANG Jonathon Green
SLEEP Steven W. Lockley and
    Russell G. Foster
SOCIAL AND CULTURAL
    ANTHROPOLOGY
    John Monaghan and Peter Just
SOCIAL PSYCHOLOGY Richard J. Crisp
SOCIAL WORK Sally Holland and
    Jonathan Scourfield
SOCIALISM Michael Newman
SOCIOLINGUISTICS John Edwards
SOCIOLOGY Steve Bruce
SOCRATES C. C. W. Taylor
SOUND Mike Goldsmith
SOUTHEAST ASIA James R. Rush
THE SOVIET UNION Stephen Lovell
THE SPANISH CIVIL WAR
    Helen Graham
SPANISH LITERATURE Jo Labanyi
SPINOZA Roger Scruton
SPIRITUALITY Philip Sheldrake
SPORT Mike Cronin
STARS Andrew King
STATISTICS David J. Hand
STEM CELLS Jonathan Slack
STOICISM Brad Inwood
STRUCTURAL ENGINEERING
    David Blockley
STUART BRITAIN John Morrill
SUPERCONDUCTIVITY
    Stephen Blundell
SUPERSTITION Stuart Vyse
SYMMETRY Ian Stewart
SYNAESTHESIA Julia Simner
SYNTHETIC BIOLOGY Jamie A. Davies
SYSTEMS BIOLOGY Eberhard O. Voit
TAXATION Stephen Smith
TEETH Peter S. Ungar
TELESCOPES Geoff Cottrell

TERRORISM Charles Townshend
THEATRE Marvin Carlson
THEOLOGY David F. Ford
THINKING AND REASONING
    Jonathan St B. T. Evans
THOMAS AQUINAS Fergus Kerr
THOUGHT Tim Bayne
TIBETAN BUDDHISM
    Matthew T. Kapstein
TIDES David George Bowers and
    Emyr Martyn Roberts
TOCQUEVILLE Harvey C. Mansfield
TOPOLOGY Richard Earl
TRAGEDY Adrian Poole
TRANSLATION Matthew Reynolds
THE TREATY OF VERSAILLES
    Michael S. Neiberg
TRIGONOMETRY
    Glen Van Brummelen
THE TROJAN WAR Eric H. Cline
TRUST Katherine Hawley
THE TUDORS John Guy
TWENTIETH-CENTURY BRITAIN
    Kenneth O. Morgan
TYPOGRAPHY Paul Luna
THE UNITED NATIONS
    Jussi M. Hanhimäki
UNIVERSITIES AND COLLEGES
    David Palfreyman and Paul Temple
THE U.S. CONGRESS Donald A. Ritchie

THE U.S. CONSTITUTION
    David J. Bodenhamer
THE U.S. SUPREME COURT
    Linda Greenhouse
UTILITARIANISM
    Katarzyna de Lazari-Radek and
    Peter Singer
UTOPIANISM Lyman Tower Sargent
VETERINARY SCIENCE James Yeates
THE VIKINGS Julian D. Richards
VIRUSES Dorothy H. Crawford
VOLTAIRE Nicholas Cronk
WAR AND TECHNOLOGY
    Alex Roland
WATER John Finney
WAVES Mike Goldsmith
WEATHER Storm Dunlop
THE WELFARE STATE David Garland
WILLIAM SHAKESPEARE
    Stanley Wells
WITCHCRAFT Malcolm Gaskill
WITTGENSTEIN A. C. Grayling
WORK Stephen Fineman
WORLD MUSIC Philip Bohlman
THE WORLD TRADE
    ORGANIZATION Amrita Narlikar
WORLD WAR II Gerhard L. Weinberg
WRITING AND SCRIPT
    Andrew Robinson
ZIONISM Michael Stanislawski

Available soon:

SMELL Matthew Cobb
THE SUN Philip Judge
DEMENTIA Kathleen Taylor

NUMBER THEORY Robin Wilson
FIRE Andrew C. Scott

For more information visit our website

www.oup.com/vsi/

Christian Reus-Smit

INTERNATIONAL
RELATIONS

A Very Short Introduction

OXFORD
UNIVERSITY PRESS

Great Clarendon Street, Oxford, OX2 6DP,
United Kingdom

Oxford University Press is a department of the University of Oxford.
It furthers the University's objective of excellence in research, scholarship,
and education by publishing worldwide. Oxford is a registered trade mark of
Oxford University Press in the UK and in certain other countries

Published in the United States of America by Oxford University Press
198 Madison Avenue, New York, NY 10016, United States of America

British Library Cataloguing in Publication Data
Data available

Library of Congress Control Number: 2020930609

ISBN 978-0-19-885021-2

Printed and bound by
CPI Group (UK) Ltd, Croydon, CR0 4YY

The manufacturer's authorised representative in the EU for product
safety is Oxford University Press España S.A. of el Parque Empresarial
San Fernando de Henares, Avenida de Castilla,
2 – 28830 Madrid (www.oup.es/en).

For Heather

Contents

Acknowledgements xvii

List of illustrations xix

List of maps xxi

List of abbreviations xxiii

1 What is international relations? 1

2 The global organization of political authority 11

3 Theory is your friend 29

4 War 47

5 Economy 64

6 Rights 83

7 Culture 102

8 An essential political science 119

Glossary 125

References 129

Further reading 137

Index 141

Acknowledgements

In writing this little book I have incurred some big debts.
At Oxford University Press, I thank Andrea Keegan for inviting
me to take on the project, Jenny Nugee for her guidance and
support in shepherding me through the production process, and
Dominic Byatt for encouraging me through the writing with his
characteristic enthusiasm: I can't thank him enough for the
detailed and immensely helpful feedback he gave on each draft
chapter. I am also grateful to my friends and colleagues Kate
Sullivan de Estrada, Shahar Hameiri, and Nicholas Wheeler
for their efforts reading parts or all of the manuscript and
providing—as always—fabulously insightful feedback.

The book was written while I was on sabbatical from the
University of Queensland, and I thank the Faculty of Humanities
and Social Sciences for supporting this leave, and my colleagues in
the School of Political Science and International Studies for
carrying my vacated responsibilities. Thanks in particular to
Katharine Gelber, Jacinta O'Hagan, Sarah Percy, Andrew Phillips,
and Heloise Weber.

Several chapters were drafted while I was a Visiting Scholar at
Nuffield College of the University of Oxford. There are few places
in the world so conducive to quiet thinking and writing, as well as
stimulating conversations with extraordinary scholars. I am

immensely grateful to Janina Dill, Andrew Hurrell, and Duncan Snidal for arranging my visit, and to the Nuffield professional staff whose efforts make college life possible. I also thank participants in the Nuffield College International Relations Seminar who read the first three chapters and offered excellent comments and suggestions.

This is the first time I've had the opportunity to thank my two children—Lili and Sam—for reading a draft of one of my books, in this case to reassure me that it was intelligible to interested but uninitiated young readers. It was an honour to have you two on board!

My greatest debt is to my partner, Heather Rae, to whom the book is dedicated. She too provided invaluable feedback on the manuscript, and this itself earns plenty of gratitude. My thanks go deeper than this, though. This book is an *introduction* to international relations, and Heather is a master at introducing this fascinating domain of politics. For twenty years I have watched her nurture students' knowledge and understanding, and seen how a well-crafted introduction can enthuse and inspire. In writing this small book, I have tried, however successfully, to take a leaf from her much larger book.

List of illustrations

1   Ambrogio Lorenzetti, *Allegory of Good Government* **4**
    Alto Vintage Images / Alamy Stock Photo.

2   War to uphold the rules of international society: the 'Highway of Death', Iraq 1991 **55**
    Danita Delimont / Alamy Stock Photo.

3   *Tipu's Tiger*: late 18th century **57**
    *Tipu's Tiger, c.*1790, Indian School. Victoria & Albert Museum, London, UK / Bridgeman Images.

4   Queen Victoria on British East Africa Protectorate coin, 1898 **67**
    Yaroslaff / Shutterstock.com.

5   Mahatma Gandhi spinning **70**
    gandhiserve.org / Wikimedia Commons / Public Domain.

6   The 'Boomerang Pattern' of transnational influence **96**
    Adapted with permission from Thomas Risse, Stephen C. Ropp, and Kathryn Sikkink, et al. (eds.), *The Power of Human Rights: International Norms and Domestic Change* (Cambridge: Cambridge University Press, 1999).

7   The 'Spiral Model' of human rights change **98**
    Adapted with permission from Thomas Risse, Stephen C. Ropp, and Kathryn Sikkink, et al. (eds.), *The Power of Human Rights: International Norms and Domestic Change* (Cambridge: Cambridge University Press, 1999).

List of maps

1   Contemporary political
    map of Europe **18**
    ekler / Shutterstock.com.

2   The world's empires in
    1900 **21**

3   The Catalan map of the
    medieval Mediterranean:
    1200 **23**
    The Picture Art Collection / Alamy
    Stock Photo.

List of abbreviations

ANZUS	The Australia, New Zealand, United States Security Treaty
AU	African Union
CAT	Convention against Torture and Other Cruel, Inhumane or Degrading Treatment
CEDAW	Convention to End Discrimination Against Women
CPPCG	Convention on the Prevention and Punishment of the Crime of Genocide
CPTPP	Comprehensive and Progressive Agreement for Trans-Pacific Partnership
CRC	Convention on the Rights of the Child
ECHR	European Convention on Human Rights
EU	European Union
G20	Group of Twenty
GATT	General Agreement on Tariffs and Trade
GDP	gross domestic product
GFC	Global Financial Crisis
ICC	International Criminal Court
ICCPR	International Convention on Civil and Political Rights
ICESCR	International Covenant on Economic, Social and Cultural Rights

ICTY	International Criminal Tribunal for the Former Yugoslavia
IMF	International Monetary Fund
INGO	International Non-Governmental Organization
ISIL	Islamic State of Iraq and the Levant
LGBTQI	lesbian, gay, bisexual, transgender, queer, and intersex
NGO	Non-Governmental Organization
NIEO	New International Economic Order
NPT	Nuclear Non-Proliferation Treaty
OECD	Organization for Economic Co-operation and Development
OPEC	Organization of Petroleum Exporting Countries
PPP	Purchasing Price Parity
R2P	Responsibility to Protect
RCTR	International Criminal Tribunal for Rwanda
UN	United Nations
UNESCO	United Nations Educational, Scientific, and Cultural Organization
UNFCCC	United Nations Framework Convention on Climate Change
UNHCR	United Nations High Commissioner for Refugees
UNSC	United Nations Security Council
WTO	World Trade Organization
WWI	World War One
WWII	World War Two

International Relations

Chapter 1
What is international relations?

Let's start with some key events. In 2019 Hong Kong's citizens waged months of mass protests against the erosion of their democratic rights, and that September an estimated six million people across the world took to the streets in a global strike for urgent action on climate change. In 2016 the British people voted to leave the European Union (EU) and Donald Trump was elected President of the United States (US). In 2008 the Global Financial Crisis (GFC) wreaked havoc in the world economy, and seven years earlier Al Qaeda terrorists attacked the US, sparking the ongoing global 'war on terror'. In 1989 protestors in East and West Germany pulled down the Berlin Wall and helped bring an end to the long 'Cold War' between the Soviet Union and the US. In 1966 the United Nations (UN) adopted the two most important human rights treaties: the Covenants on 'Civil and Political Rights' and 'Cultural, Economic, and Social Rights'. In 1955 leaders of newly independent post-colonial states (such as China, Egypt, and India) met in Bandung, Indonesia, to fight for an end to empire and for a new international order based on political, economic, and cultural equality. The first half of the 20th century was, of course, dominated by World War One (WWI), the Great Depression of the 1930s, and World War Two (WWII). And in 1945 the UN was established in the hope that international cooperation and governance would prevent a return to war, stabilize the world economy, and protect human rights.

All of these events fall within the grand domain of international relations. But if this is the case, what is international relations? How can such diverse phenomena all come within its ambit? Scholars of international relations have traditionally focused on external relations between sovereign states: wars, trade negotiations, arms control, environmental treaties, etc. And these remain critical subjects of inquiry. Yet the limits of this focus are readily apparent. Not all important relations are between sovereign states: the war on terror, after all, is between state and non-state actors. Not all important politics is external: Brexit and Donald Trump's presidency show just how important domestic phenomena can be well beyond the borders of a single state. And if international relations is truly only about the affairs of sovereign states, then our subject matter will be very limited, as today's *global* system of sovereign states emerged fully only with post-1945 decolonization. Before that sovereign states certainly existed, principally in Europe and the Americas, but as we shall see it was empires that ruled most of the world.

Given all of this, some scholars say we should address the broader subject of 'global politics', arguing that the concept of 'international relations' is too narrow to accommodate the rich diversity of important political phenomena. Yet this goes too far. If politics is about struggles for power, or about who gets what, when, and how, if it spans the public and private realms, and if it is a defining characteristic of all human associations—all things said about politics—then the content of global politics is potentially limitless. Where would we start, and where would we end, in describing such politics?

This *Very Short Introduction* takes a different approach. Raymond Aron, the great French historian and international relations scholar, wrote that '"International Relations" have no frontiers traced out in reality, they are not and cannot be materially separable from other social phenomena'. What he meant is that 'international relations' is a concept that scholars, practitioners, commentators, and people in their everyday lives use to define a particular domain of social life, a domain they imagine and construct through their actions. So if the traditional imagining of the international is too narrow, and 'global politics' too broad, what should be our focus? My big claim in this little book is that we should focus on the global organization of political authority, and on the human and environmental consequences of such organization.

Political authority is legitimate political power. It is power that is considered rightful. It is the form of political power that Ambrogio Lorenzetti, the early Renaissance artist, sought to capture in his famous Sienese fresco, the 'Allegory of Good Government' (see Figure 1). Lorenzetti portrays the male figure of the legitimate ruler as tied to the citizenry and surrounded by female figures representing the civic virtues of justice, concord, magnanimity, temperance, peace, fortitude, and prudence. Such a ruler, Lorenzetti writes at the bottom of the fresco, 'chooses never to turn his eyes from the resplendent faces of the Virtues who sit around him' (quoted in Starn). This is, of course, a thoroughly gendered illustration of political authority (a point I return to Chapter 3), but it offers nonetheless a particularly stark depiction of the differences between political authority and tyranny (political power that rests solely on coercion). These 14th-century frescos are interesting not just because they help us grasp the nature of political authority as legitimate power, but because Lorenzetti painted them as an act of legitimation. Not all political power is legitimate: coercive domination exists all too often. But Lorenzetti's artistic act embodies the abiding impulse to justify power, to turn domination into political authority.

How political authority is organized has profound implications for human societies and—as we are increasingly aware—for the natural environments they inhabit. Think about sovereign states. They are now the dominant way of organizing political authority on the globe, centralizing legitimate political power within

1. Ambrogio Lorenzetti, *Allegory of Good Government.*

distinct, territorially bounded units. This affects individuals' rights (some states are authoritarian, others democracies), the functioning of economies (some states have command economies, others are more liberal), the provision of health and education services (some states have well-funded welfare systems, others do not), the diversity and inclusivity of cultural communities (some states are multicultural, others strongly nationalistic), and the protection or exploitation of nature (some states are 'greener' than others). Just as importantly, the division of the world into almost 200 separate sovereign states generates its own pathologies—from interstate war to refugee crises—while at the same time placing real limits on humanity's capacity to address such problems.

Throughout history humans have experienced the organization of political authority most palpably at local levels, in their villages, tribes, municipalities, colonies, city-states, provinces, and nation-states. But these local authorities have usually been embedded in larger regional, imperial, interstate, transnational, and supranational configurations of political authority. For example, Native American tribes were often part of larger confederacies, such as the Iroquois League, which included the Mohawk, Oneida, Onondaga, Cayuga, and Seneca nations. Similarly, until the 19th century, although Japan, Korea, and Vietnam were distinct polities, with their own dynasties and imperial domains, they were also at times part of a larger Chinese suzerain order, and as part of this they paid tribute to Chinese emperors. Today, sovereign states are legally independent but they are embedded in a global system of states, with distinctive challenges, institutions, and political practices. When I call for a focus on the 'global' organization of political authority, I am referring to these larger configurations, regardless of whether they span the earth or not. Indeed, today's system of sovereign states may be the only genuinely global case.

Two things make this current way of organizing political authority especially fascinating. The first is its novelty. Students of international relations were long taught to assume a world organized into sovereign states, and to study its eternal verities: its tendency to 'recurrence and repetition', as the leading English School theorist Martin Wight observed. As noted above, though, prior to the 1970s the majority of humans lived in polities that were not sovereign states, most commonly in empires. The development of a system of sovereign states that spanned the entire globe was something utterly new, and it is a very recent development. This raises intriguing questions about its origins, dynamics, consequences, and potential transformation, questions that the system's novelty makes all the more challenging. Second, today's global configuration of authority is highly complex. Political authority is not simply parcelled up into multiple sovereign states—it is also invested in supranational bodies (like the EU), international organizations (such as the UN), and transnational actors (like multinational corporations). Moreover, politics within sovereign states is often deeply affected by these 'external' authorities. For example, states have given international human rights bodies, like the office of the United Nations High Commissioner for Refugees (UNHCR), the authority to report on the treatment of refugees, often challenging the policies and behaviour of national governments and empowering local and transnational activists.

Placing the global organization of political authority at the heart of our inquiries invites both analytical and ethical questions. Analytically, we can ask how political authority came to be organized in a particular way, we can probe its political dynamics and consequences (from the violent to the humane), and we can explore the forces driving its evolution and transformation. We can also ask how different historical arrangements of political authority compare, and how one transformed over time into another (how today's global system of states emerged from the collapse of the Chinese, European, Mughal, and Ottoman empires, for example). And, most importantly, we can ask how large-scale ways of organizing political authority have at times fostered human well-being but also produced hierarchies and exclusions: of race, gender, religion, sexuality, caste, and more.

This *Very Short Introduction* concentrates on analytical questions such these, but ethical questions also follow naturally from a focus on the organization of political authority. If such authority is rightful power, then it is always in part the product of historical debates and struggles over the good served by that power: the justice it delivers, the rights it protects, the morality it upholds. These debates are central to contemporary international relations: what are the limits of sovereign authority, when should human rights be protected, does the international community have a responsibility to protect peoples from mass atrocities, should reducing inequality be a goal of global economic governance, what obligations do we have to address the climate emergency, and what is more fundamental, the right to asylum or the right to police national borders? Not only is it appropriate that students of international relations address such questions, doing so is essential if we wish to speak to some of the most pressing issues of our time.

In the following chapters, I introduce international relations through the lens of the global organization of political authority. Chapter 2 examines such organization more closely, and provides a brief overview of some of the most prominent historical forms: heteronomy (think of feudal Europe), empire (from the Moghul to the British), and sovereignty (at its apogee, perhaps, in today's global system). My goals are twofold. I emphasize, first, the nature and importance of institutions, understood broadly as formal or informal systems of rules, norms, and practices. These range from underlying norms of sovereignty to the rules governing international trade. Such institutions are important, as they play a crucial role in organizing political authority. My second goal is to place today's global system of sovereign states in a broader conceptual and historical framework, encouraging readers to see it as but one crucially important yet utterly unique way of ordering social and political life.

Chapter 3 takes a theoretical turn. You might hear that theory is an academic indulgence. 'What we want', as Charles Dickens's schoolmaster Thomas Gradgrind insisted, 'is facts, nothing but facts, weed everything else out'. In reality, however, theory is an indispensable ally to understanding, and the idea of theory-free inquiry is an unhelpful myth. Theories are nothing more than organized assumptions that help us make sense of complexity, and even the most 'factual' accounts of international relations reflect such assumptions, informing which facts the authors thought were important: the personalities and choices of great leaders, the ideas or culture of the time, the distribution of material power, the role of capitalism, etc. As students of international relations it makes sense for us to be reflective and systematic in our use of such assumptions, and the principal way we do this is by organizing them into theories. To help with this task, I introduce readers to some of the most prominent existing theories of international relations, from realism to feminism. I read these differently than is common, however. I resist the common practice of dividing them into 'analytical' and 'ethical' theories, or 'mainstream' and 'critical' theories, and argue instead that all are centrally concerned with how political authority is defined and distributed globally, and with what consequences.

Powerful social forces have shaped—and been shaped by—the large-scale organization of political authority over time, and Chapters 4 to 7 explore some of the most important: war, economy, rights, and culture. Throughout history, war has had a profound effect on structures and practices of political authority. Think of how WWI swept away the Austro-Hungarian, German, and Ottoman empires. Chapter 4 defines war as purposive, organized violence, and examines how shifting patterns of such violence have generated forms of political authority, served as a key marker of such authority, and been objects of political and legal control.

Chapter 5 turns to the relationship between economies and the organization of political authority, arguing that the two are mutually dependent. After considering three shifting conditions—changes in the global economy, revolutions in technology, and shifts in the global distribution of economic resources—it examines key developments in the organization of political authority, and how these have affected global economic relations.

All arrangements of political authority define and distribute rights. Contemporary states grant certain rights to citizens, while denying them to non-citizens, such as refugees. Similarly, in empires, the citizens of imperial states commonly enjoyed one set of rights, while colonial subjects had different, lesser entitlements. Since 1945 international human rights treaties have codified the rights of all humans, simultaneously investing international human rights rules and agencies with authority while limiting the sovereign rights of states. In each of these cases, the nature and distribution of rights has affected the scope and limits of political authority. Chapter 6 examines two dimensions of the politics of rights: the role that individual rights played in the emergence of today's global system of sovereign states; and how local struggles for human rights, connected to the transnational human rights movement, have sought to redefine and limit sovereign authority.

The final factor we consider is culture. The rise of non-Western great powers, especially China, raises important questions about how culture affects the global organization of political authority. While some predict that the modern international order will collapse as Western cultural influence wanes, and others counter that liberal international institutions can accommodate states and peoples of diverse cultural complexions, Chapter 7 presents a different view. Historically, all large-scale configurations of political authority have evolved in heterogeneous not homogeneous cultural contexts, and the forms they have taken—the institutions they develop, the hierarchies they create, and the rights they distribute—have been deeply affected by the imperative to govern or rule this diversity.

By focusing on the contests and struggles that have shaped the organization of legitimate political power, and by directing our attention to the large-scale arrangements of political authority that affect politics more locally, the study of international relations confronts directly the fundamental political conditions of global social and biological life. This is political science at its most fascinating (and arguably most important), and this *Very Short Introduction* invites readers to view their world, and the profound challenges it faces, through this unique and illuminating lens.

Chapter 2
The global organization of political authority

If you doubt that the study of international relations ought to focus on the global organization of political authority think about these issues: Britain's withdrawal from the EU, the struggle over territorial and maritime rights in the South China Sea, the failed attempt by the Islamic State of Iraq and the Levant (ISIL) to establish a new caliphate on Iraqi and Syrian territories, the US withdrawal from the Paris Climate Agreement, Japan's departure from the International Whaling Association and resumption of commercial whaling, the rights that multinational corporations have sought to sue states for losses caused by national environmental regulations, and the Russian rejection of international norms of sexual non-discrimination. Every one of these is centrally—and essentially—concerned with the nature and distribution of political authority. All involve struggles for power, but time and again it is political authority, or legitimate power, that is at stake. Should Britain have to abide by European rules and regulations? Does China have historical rights to control large swathes of the South China Sea or should the Law of the Sea define the rights of littoral states? Is it legitimate for religious insurgents to destroy existing sovereign states in the Middle East and institute their conception of a classical Islamic polity? Should multilateral agreements define how states respond to climate change? Are states still sovereign if non-state actors have the right to sue them for their legislative actions? Should there be international norms that prohibit sexual discrimination? These are not just academic questions, they animate some of the most heated controversies in contemporary international relations.

A striking thing about all of these issues is that they only make sense in a world where political authority is organized on the principle of sovereignty (which holds that the state has supreme authority within its borders and need recognize no higher authority beyond those borders). Since the 1970s almost the entire globe has been divided into territorial states, each claiming sovereign authority. As we shall see, states have invested authority in international institutions and organizations, like the African Union (AU) and the World Trade Organization (WTO). But if sovereign rights were not considered primary, Brexiteers would have had nothing to campaign for, China's expansive maritime claims would be less controversial, there would be no order of sovereign states in the Middle East for ISIL to threaten, the Paris Climate Agreement could not be presented as an attack on US independence, and handing legal rights to multilateral corporations would be less controversial. Yet for most of world history this is *not* how political authority has been organized globally. Regional systems of states have existed in the past: in Ancient and Classical Greece (800 to at least 300 BC), China in the 'Warring States' period (475–221 BC), India before the Mauryan Empire (321–185 BC), and in Renaissance Italy (1350–1500 AD). But these were very different from today's global system, and they were unusual moments in a broader history dominated by empires, feudal configurations of authority, or some combination of these.

As argued in Chapter 1, it is the uniqueness—not naturalness—of today's global system of sovereign states that makes it so fascinating. But to grasp this uniqueness we have to understand, first, how it differs from other historical ways of organizing political authority; and, second, how it emerged only very recently. This chapter serves these purposes, contrasting three historical ways of organizing political authority (sovereignty, empire, and heteronomy), and providing a brief account of the emergence of today's global order. Before we can get to these tasks, however, we need to consider the nature and function of institutions. As we will see in the following chapters, a host of factors affect how political authority is defined and distributed, from war to culture. But whatever these factors might be, arrangements of political authority—small- and large-scale—are always held together by institutions. These can be confusing things, though, and my first task is to explain what institutions are and the different forms they take.

Institutions

Elsewhere I define institutions as sets of norms, rules, and practices that shape actors' identities and regulate their behaviour. There is a venerable 'realist' tradition of thinking about international relations that denies the importance of institutions. What matters, realists say, is material power (principally guns and money), and rules and norms only exist and have any effect when great powers want them to. Material might does, of course, have a big impact on international relations, but the realist view sits uncomfortably with the sheer centrality of institutions to everyday life. At the most fundamental level, most of today's sovereign states survive not because they have the material power to repel aggressive predator states, but in part because they have sovereign rights, backed by a cardinal international norm that sovereignty must be respected. The very existence of materially weak states depends, therefore, on an institution. States also devote an enormous amount of time and energy to institutional politics: to creating new institutions, arguing over their rights and obligations, and, far more than realists credit, complying with institutional rules and norms. Furthermore, as the examples above indicate, many of today's most heated conflicts and controversies hinge on the relative importance of different institutions: sovereignty versus supranational rules (Brexit), historic rights versus international law (China's claims in the South China Sea), and multilateral rules versus the constitutional authority of national lawmakers (the failed first version of the Trans-Pacific Partnership).

Institutions vary in several ways. They can be formal, as when rules and norms are codified in law, or they can be informal, expressed simply in shared understandings. The UN Charter and Britain's 'special relationship' with the US are both institutions, but the first is formal, the latter largely informal. Sometimes institutions are constructed by design, as in the case of the Charter, but they can also evolve more incrementally, through the routine practices of actors. The institution of diplomacy—so central to international relations—is a good example. The Italian city-states first deployed resident ambassadors in the 14th century, but there was no founding moment of diplomacy: it evolved through several distinct forms over the course of the next seven centuries, with accepted practices gradually being codified.

The biggest mistake students make is confusing institutions and organizations. Leading scholar of international relations John Ruggie argues that organizations are bureaucratic entities 'with headquarters and letterheads', whereas institutions are just rules, norms, and practices, formal or informal. Organizations always rest on underlying institutions: for example, the UN (an organization) is founded on its Charter (an institution). Institutions often exist without associated organizations, however. The ANZUS Treaty between Australia, New Zealand, and the US is a formal institution, but there is no ANZUS organization. Sometimes institutions develop organizational dimensions over time. The best example is the WTO, which started life as the 1948 General Agreement on Tariffs and Trade (GATT), an international treaty with little if any organizational architecture.

When thinking about international institutions it is useful to distinguish between three different types. The institutions we are most familiar with—the ones we hear most about in the media—are commonly called 'issue-specific institutions' or 'international regimes'. As the name suggests, these institutions are usually created to address specific functional challenges, like nuclear arms control or managing global postal services. The number of such institutions greatly increased from the 19th century onward, and there are now thousands of them. Some of the most famous are the Nuclear Non-Proliferation Treaty (NPT), the UN Framework Convention on Climate Change (UNFCCC), the Convention to End Discrimination Against Women (CEDAW), the Rome Statute of the International Criminal Court, the International Covenant on Civil and Political Rights (ICCPR), and the Ottawa Convention on Anti-Personnel Landmines. Sometimes these institutions reflect the leadership of powerful states, as did the wave of institutions created after WWII (the UN, the International Monetary Fund (IMF), the World Bank, etc.). Sometimes they reflect an awareness on the part of a broad range of states that there are challenges they can only address collectively. And sometimes they reflect the persistent campaigning of non-state actors, from transnational human rights networks to multinational corporations.

Whatever their origins, issue-specific institutions are not free standing: they express a deeper, less apparent, form of institutions. Elsewhere I term these 'fundamental institutions' or 'basic institutional practices'. Think about the examples above. When states negotiated these regimes they did two things: they created international law and they engaged in multilateralism (cooperation between three or more states). In other words, they addressed diverse challenges by enacting a small repertoire of long accepted institutional practices. Historically, the practices favoured by states and other political actors have varied greatly. Modern forms of international law and multilateralism rose to prominence in the 19th century, but before that older practices of law and diplomacy prevailed among European states (and these were expressed still differently in the ruling of their overseas empires). The Ancient Greeks had no notions of international law or multilateralism, but had an advanced system of interstate arbitration. The Renaissance Italians pioneered interstate diplomacy, but this was a very different diplomacy to our modern form.

Below all of this lies a third level of institutions, usefully termed 'constitutional'. The best way to understand these is to think about the legal constitutions of sovereign states. Among other things, constitutions define how political authority is distributed within a state. They specify the legitimate political and legal entities: the executive, the legislature, and the courts, for example. They determine how these stand in relation to one another, and how they work to make legitimate rules and decisions. They may also stipulate the relationship between the state and the citizenry, specifying the rights of both and thus the nature and scope of political authority. Put differently, constitutions define the rules of the political game: who are the legitimate actors, and what are their legitimate powers. Large-scale configurations of political authority—such as empires and systems of sovereign states—seldom have formal constitutions (although some think that the UN Charter approximates one). They always rest, however, on informal constitutional norms: on shared understandings about which are the legitimate political authorities, what is the scope of their authority, and how they stand in relation to one another. Today's global system of sovereign states is a good example. When states invoke their sovereign rights, they do not do this in an institutional vacuum. They do so within a clearly understood framework of constitutional norms, which define states as the principal units of political authority, give them certain rights (like making laws and self-defence), and specify that they are legal equals, regardless of their material inequalities. Sovereignty is thus a constitutional institution, and other levels of institutions—fundamental and issue-specific—presuppose its existence.

Three maps

One of the best means of introducing different historical ways of organizing political authority is through maps. Two words of caution are needed, however. First, maps have been made for different purposes, and even when they give insights into the organization of political authority, this has not always been their primary purpose. Medieval maps, for example, were most often designed for navigation and the linear plotting of pilgrimage or trade routes. Second, we now know that cartography—the art and science of map-making—has not simply been a tool of representation, doing nothing more than documenting, in visual form, how political authority has been distributed. To the contrary, emerging cartographic technologies made it possible for rulers to imagine political authority in particular ways. For example, as Jordan Branch, the pioneering scholar in this area, explains, territorial sovereignty was only conceivable after the cartographic revolution of the Renaissance enabled the accurate mapping of physical space, allowing it to be divided and demarcated.

With these cautions noted, three maps provide useful starting points for grasping different historical ways of configuring authority on a large scale. Let us begin with a contemporary political map of Europe (Map 1). Here we see the political world assumed in standard accounts of international relations: a world divided into territorially demarcated sovereign states. Each state is easily identified, as it has distinct boundaries that separate it from other states. What is it, though, that these boundaries divide? We might stand on any of them and see no physical differences between one side and the other, the people inhabiting the border regions might even speak the same languages. What these boundaries separate is the political authority of one sovereign state from another. The constitutional norm of sovereignty gives states supreme authority within their territories,

Map 1. Contemporary political map of Europe.

and this map provides a graphic representation of this way of organizing political authority. Where the authority of France stops and that of Germany begins is clearly visible.

As well as illustrating how political authority is distributed in a system of sovereign states, the map reveals something deeper: the institutional foundations of this distribution—the fact that sovereignty is a system-wide constitutional norm. Note how the map depicts not only political giants like Germany, France, and the UK, but also tiny states like Luxembourg and Monaco. These states exist and survive not because they have the military might to defend their independence, but because they are recognized as sovereign states, with rights to non-intervention, self-determination, and diplomatic standing. Also note that the territorial boundary between Luxembourg and Germany is as definitive and absolute as that between Germany and France. As far as formal sovereign authority goes, the map depicts all states as equals—as does the principle of sovereignty.

Of course all of this is the product of politics, often violent politics. WWII was a near terminal battle over the organization of political authority, with the principle of sovereignty contested not only by Germany's bid for primacy in Europe and North Africa and Japan's imperial campaign in Asia, but also by the continued commitment of Europe's 'sovereigns' to their empires abroad. The current sovereign order portrayed by the map did not even emerge after the war ended. Post-war borders in Western and Eastern Europe were not recognized formally until the 1975 Helsinki Accords, and many of the sovereign states now depicted gained independence only with the breakdown of the former Yugoslavia and Soviet Union. What this shows, however, is the gradual consolidation of the constitutional norm of sovereignty, resulting in the map's seemingly natural way of representing political authority. Yet this naturalness is belied by contemporary politics, most notably by the controversy and upheaval of Brexit, where the EU—a decades long project to foster peace, economic growth, and human rights through integration and supranational authority—is challenged by calls for the reassertion of a more categorical form of British sovereignty and exclusivist conception of national identity.

If this suggests that a world organized into sovereign states should not be assumed, then our second map confirms this. Map 2 is also a political map, but although it depicts global political organization only a century before Map 1, this organization could not be more different. It presents a world of sprawling empires, not sovereign states. By showing them as undifferentiated territorial blocks, it obscures important features of empires as forms of political organization: that they varied greatly in how politically centralized or decentralized they were (the British, Ottoman, and Qing empires were very different), and that fluid and diffuse imperial frontiers were as common as clear territorial boundaries. The map also hides the fact that the imperial powers at the centre of many of these empires (Britain, France, Russia, the US) related to one another as sovereign states: operating, as international relations scholar Edward Keene explains, by one set of principles between them, and another in their relations with subject peoples. Yet the map does highlight important aspects of this very different global organization of political authority. It shows the sheer scale of these empires, and as a consequence, how few of them divided up the world (only sixteen are pictured). Just as importantly, it shows how accepted empire was as a legitimate form of political organization, at least in the imperial heartlands. We often focus on the European empires, which expanded rapidly in the late 19th century, but in 1900 empire was a Chinese, Japanese, Russian, and US enterprise as well.

This world of empires had its own distinctive politics. To be sure, political struggles were ever-present, often fuelling violent conflicts. But this politics is not fruitfully reduced to 'interstate' relations alone. Such relations were central, of course. The Hague Conferences of 1899 and 1906, where European states negotiated

Austria-Hungary
Belgium
Denmark
France
Germany
Great Britain
Italy
Japan
Netherlands
Norway
Portugal
Qing Dynasty
Russia
Spain
Ottoman Turk
United States
Independent states

Map 2. The world's empires in 1900.

many of the early laws of war and laid the institutional foundations for the League of Nations and UN, testify to this. Yet the political dynamics of the world of empires was far more complex than this. The politics—and the violence—of the 19th century were driven to a large degree by imperial expansion, as European powers extended their influence and rule across Africa, Asia, and the Pacific. This not only destroyed or subjugated numerous non-Western polities, it brought Western and non-Western empires into direct conflict (Britain's Opium Wars with China being a key example). Even when sovereign states were building institutions that we now identify as 'interstate'—existing for states, between states—the imperatives of empire drove much of what they did. It is now well-documented that the fundamental institution of international law evolved, in significant measure, to serve the ends of empire. It was in international law that the notorious 'standard of civilization' was codified, providing Western powers with the legal criteria on which to grant or deny sovereignty to non-Western peoples. Similarly, key issue-specific institutions of the time were designed to meet the functional challenges that attended the age of imperialism. For example, the General Act of the 1885 Berlin Conference set out rules to prevent European powers conflicting as they raced for colonial acquisitions in their 'Scramble for Africa'.

The differences between the large-scale organizations of political authority depicted in Maps 1 and 2 are marked, yet they differ again from that portrayed in Map 3: the medieval 'Catalan' map of the Mediterranean in roughly 1200. This is a classic example of a 'Portolan' chart, designed principally to assist sailors with navigation. But while its main purpose was not political representation, it reveals something striking about political organization at the time: there are no sovereign states—no territorial boundaries are marked at all. It shows numerous coastal towns, as well as important inland cities and routes of travel. It also has images along the bottom of throned rulers, and even a tented army. But there is no way to identify the political

Map 3. The Catalan map of the medieval Mediterranean: 1200.

jurisdictions of these rulers: what they rule over and where. This is not just because of the limits of available cartographic technologies: it reflects the actual nature of the medieval organization of political authority. This was a 'heteronomous' world, where there were multiple centres of authority: local lords, towns and cities, regional monarchies, loosely integrated empires, and Catholic, Byzantine, and Islamic religious authorities. None of these had exclusive territorially demarcated authority: their political and legal jurisdictions overlapped, multiple systems of law coexisted, and the boundary between political and religious authority was opaque and contested.

Like the sovereign and imperial ways of organizing political authority, the heteronomous way generated its own distinctive politics. Again, political struggles and violent conflicts were common. But these had little to do with what we now conceive as sovereign states. The 'constitutive' wars that produced such states in Europe were still several centuries away, as was the conquest violence of the early Dutch, Portuguese, and Spanish empires. Furthermore, there was as yet no clear separation of public and private violence, and the idea of a state monopoly over violence, so central to the idea of the modern sovereign state, was a far distant idea. In the medieval world, struggles over legitimate power took at least three forms. First, key struggles revolved around which authorities had precedence over which domains of human life: the persistent struggle between the Holy Roman Emperor and the Pope over the boundaries between secular and religious authority being the principal example. Second, there were struggles over religious artefacts and symbols, often used to bolster the legitimacy of local rulers and galvanize regional political action. Think of the Crusades and the long struggle between Christians and Muslims for control of Jerusalem. Third, struggles raged over how legitimate political authority was acquired, with the claims of aspirant rulers often pushed as far as the family tree would allow (a practice that was only seriously curtailed after the 17th-century Wars of Spanish Succession). Finally, there were increasingly common struggles for political autonomy, evident first in the growing assertiveness of wealthy towns.

The genesis of the global system of states

These maps show not only some of the very different ways humans have organized political authority on a large scale, but also how very recent is today's world of sovereign states. Map 2, depicting the earth divided into empires, is dated 1900, and this political world did not collapse fully until the 1970s. What this transformation entailed, and how it occurred, shapes today's international relations in profound ways. The nature and functioning of the UN, how China understands its rights and entitlements as a rising power, global trade negotiations, the politics of intervention, the grievances and objectives of transnational insurgents (like ISIL and Al Qaeda), and more: all are products, in one form or another, of this transformation.

The rest of this chapter looks at two dimensions of the transformation from a world of empires to our present global system of sovereign states. To grasp these dimensions it is helpful to employ a famous distinction (coined by the eminent international relations scholar Robert Gilpin) between two kinds of international change: 'systemic' and 'systems' change. The first is change that occurs within a system of sovereign states: particularly, change in the distribution of power. For example, between WWI and WWII there was a 'multipolar' distribution, with power spread across five or more great powers. After 1945 this gave way to a 'bipolar' distribution, where power was concentrated in the hands of the US and the Soviet Union. This was in turn replaced after the end of the Cold War by a 'unipolar' distribution, when the US was widely considered the world's sole remaining superpower. The second form of change—systems change—is more fundamental, involving a major shift in the underlying constitutional norms of a system. As we have seen, constitutional norms are social understandings about which are the legitimate political authorities, what they can rightfully do, and how they stand in relation to one another. Until recently, international relations scholars showed little interest in this kind of change, as they took for granted a world organized into sovereign states. As soon as we realize that this world is very new, however, systems change leaps to the fore.

Systemic change is often conceived narrowly as shifts in the distribution of material power: guns and money, principally. But change within a system of states involves more than this. Importantly for our purposes, over the past century the gradually expanding system of sovereign states—embedded for much of this time in a wider configuration of empires—saw significant internal shifts in the organization of political authority. Two of these stand out. The first involves shifting patterns of political hegemony—the recognized authority of a leading state or hegemon. Although sovereign states are formally legal equals, systems of states also develop accepted forms of hierarchy, of which political hegemony is the most important. Shifting patterns of such hegemony are important because hegemons have historically played leading roles in defining the rules and norms governing international relations. The most commonly cited example is the role that the US played in developing post-1945 institutions (discussed further in Chapter 5): the UN, the global economic institutions (the IMF, the World Bank, and the GATT), and the major human rights instruments. In the late 19th century Britain was the political hegemon, its power waning in the first half of the 20th century, eventually eclipsed by the rise of the US after WWII. While enormously influential, US political hegemony was long confined within the Western sphere of the bipolar system, only attaining global reach after the end of the Cold War in the early 1990s. The global political hegemony of the US is now in question, however, its leadership challenged by a rapidly rising China, by disgruntled states like Russia, and by a flagging will to lead at home.

The second internal (or systemic) change in the organization of political authority is the proliferation of issue-specific institutions or regimes, mentioned earlier. John Ruggie argues that systems of sovereign states, in which political authority is concentrated in the hands of territorial political units, suffer from a paradox. As soon as authority is defined as the exclusive preserve of independent states, these very same states have to 'unbundle' their authority onto international institutions in order to address non-territorial challenges. Take these examples. If sovereign states want to navigate the world's oceans peacefully—oceans that none of them owns—then they have to acknowledge the authority of laws of the sea. Likewise, if states wish to trade freely with one another, they have to treat commonly agreed trade rules as authoritative. Lastly, if states want to combat climate change—perhaps the greatest non-territorial challenge—they cannot do it simply by exercising their territorial authority: they have to coordinate their actions by negotiating authoritative international rules. None of these issues are amenable to territorial fixes. Not surprisingly, as the initially small system of sovereign states gradually spread across the globe, and as the functional challenges that came with growing independence multiplied, the number of issue-specific institutions exploded. As I have shown elsewhere, between 1648 and 1814 European states signed only 127 multilateral treaties, but between 1814 and 1914 the number jumped to 817. Since then, especially since 1945, the number has reached the tens of thousands.

While these systemic changes in hegemony and issue-specific institutions were underway, a deeper 'systems' change in world politics unfolded. In 1900 a small system of sovereign states, located principally in Europe and the Americas, was nested in a wider set of empires. Moreover, states and empires were often adjoined: Britain, France, and the US, for example, were all simultaneously sovereign states and empires. This sovereign-imperial system was the product of often violent power politics, but it was also institutionalized, held together by a distinctive set of constitutional norms. These norms legitimized sovereignty at home, in the Western core, and empire abroad, over largely non-Western peoples. Evidence of these norms can be found in the 1945 UN Charter, which upholds both the rights of recognized sovereign states and the 'sacred trust' invested in some of these states (usually imperial powers) to administer non-self-governing territories. In one of the most dramatic transformations in the global organization of political authority in world history, this sovereign-imperial system was swept away over the next three decades, replaced by the world's first global system of sovereign states.

This change has been attributed to a host of factors, from post-war weakness of Europe's imperial powers and the anti-imperial preferences of the new superpowers, the US and the Soviet Union, to the struggles of colonized peoples or the needs of modern capitalism. All arguments fail, however, unless they account for two related things: the near simultaneous collapse of Europe's great colonial empires and the breakdown of the institution of empire itself, of the millennia-old belief that empire was a legitimate way of organizing political authority. It was the second of these—the moral bankrupting of empire—that enabled the universal collapse of Europe's empires. Imperial strength varied from one empire to another, the anti-imperialism of the US waned after the start of the Cold War, and anti-colonial struggles were decisive in some colonies but not others. None of these adequately explains why all empires collapsed at once. As we will see in Chapter 6, it was the delegitimation of empire that was crucial, an achievement of a long campaign for the rights of all colonized peoples to self-determination, a campaign waged principally in the new human rights forums of the UN. The success of this campaign not only delegitimized empire (though not other forms of hierarchy or types of domination), it established state sovereignty as the prevailing principle for the organization of political authority globally. The result was a dramatic expansion in the number of recognized sovereign states, with seventy-six new states gaining independence between 1946 and 1975.

Chapter 3
Theory is your friend

Focusing on the global organization of political authority enables students of international relations to escape the limits of the traditional concern with external relations between sovereign states and provides something more specific to address than the nebulous realm of global politics. But even if less amorphous, the global organization of political authority remains complex and shifting, and might seem almost overwhelming. We can ask any number of fascinating questions about this organization, from how and why it changes over time to its relationship with organized violence and inequalities of gender, race, or ethnicity. The questions are potentially limitless, and this is what makes studying international relations so exciting. But whichever questions we choose, how are we to answer them? One response would be to begin by looking at the relevant facts. What are those facts, though? For any given question there will be a myriad available facts. How do we decide which ones are relevant? If we set out to compile a comprehensive list of all facts associated with, say, global inequality and the organization of political authority, what would we include and exclude, and among those included, how would we decide which matter most? How would we even decide which ones to investigate?

This chapter argues that theory is essential to these tasks. Indeed, theorizing is an inherent and indispensable feature of all inquiry into the social and natural worlds, not least into the complex domain of international relations. Before readers will be persuaded of this, however, we need to demystify theory—distil its essential qualities and treat it as an everyday human practice, not the preserve of select members of the academy. It is an everyday practice not because humans love abstraction or reading Chinese, French, German, or Indian philosophers (though some clearly do), but because the use of assumptions to make sense of complexity—the essence of theorizing—is necessary for navigating the social and natural worlds. Once this is understood the idea of theory-free inquiry becomes nonsensical, whether in everyday life or scholarship. The only choice we have, I argue below, is whether to be unconscious and ad hoc in our theorizing, or reflective and systematic. Since the latter is the only reasonable option, I go on to survey six prominent theoretical perspectives on international relations: realism, liberalism, constructivism, the English School, feminism, and post-colonialism. Debate between these theories does not structure the discussions of war, economy, rights, and culture that appear in following chapters, although their ideas will at certain points be readily apparent. Rather, I introduce them here as general tools of analysis, transportable aids that readers can use in comprehending international relations more generally. Historically, these theories have been divided into any number of categories, most commonly into 'mainstream' or 'problem-solving' theories, on the one hand, and 'critical' theories, on the other. For a variety of reasons, I eschew such distinctions, arguing that despite their differences these theories share something important: all are centrally concerned with the global organization of political authority.

Theories and facts

Theories take many different forms. There are formal, mathematical theories and verbal, discursive theories. There are grand theories and middle range theories. There are primarily analytical theories and largely ethical theories. There are theories that seek general social or natural laws and others that shun such ambitions. There are simple and complex theories. There are theories that lead inquiries from the front and others that lurk in the shadows. And, as I will argue, there are theories created by scholars and theories fashioned in everyday life, by everyday people. What makes all of these 'theories' is that in essence they are nothing more than organized assumptions that help us make sense of complexity. In the study of international relations, the most common assumptions concern the drivers of political behaviour. Scholars assume, somewhat divergently, that states like individuals are inherently aggressive and domineering, or that they are self-interested and strategic, or that they are driven by material interests (such as military might or economic gain), or that the absence of a world government compels states to maximize their power to preserve their security, or that state behaviour, like that of individuals, is shaped by prevailing social norms and practices. Different scholars start with different assumptions, but all build on them to make sense of the complexity they seek to understand.

While many think that theorizing is a practice confined to the academy—the questionable art of professional nerds—nothing could be further from the truth. Human beings are natural, habitual, and inescapable theorists. Theorizing—the use of assumptions to make sense of complexity—is essential to our daily lives, enabling us to comprehend and navigate the tangled, multidimensional social and natural worlds in which we live. Here are some examples. If you are invited to a new friend's house for dinner, you will make assumptions about what this means: about what having 'dinner' entails, what one wears, when to arrive and depart, what to bring, and how to behave. Without these assumptions, or if your assumptions are wrong, you will be lost in a social labyrinth. We realize the power of our assumptions most palpably when they fail us. I was once at a conference in Chicago and went out for a morning run. I needed to cross Michigan Avenue to get to the lake foreshore, so as an Australian I checked that there was no traffic approaching on my right and then started out across the road. I nearly died. Hearing the yells of other pedestrians, I looked to my left as four or five lanes of cars bore rapidly down upon me. My assumptions about how traffic moves were fundamentally wrong, and the hair on the back of my neck stood up for weeks. The assumptions we make about how the social world works are readily apparent in everyday discussions about politics. Imagine five friends sitting in a café discussing the upheavals in the Middle East. It would not be unusual to find Bella, let's say, arguing that the cause of the problem is competition between global great powers, Malik emphasizing the legacy of colonialism, Ling claiming that it's all about religion, Woodrow insisting that Arabs aren't suited to democracy, and Lila holding that only true democracy and respect for human rights can bring peace to the region. All of these positions reflect underlying assumptions about the fundamental drivers of Middle Eastern politics, and how they stand in relative importance.

Historians have much to say of value about how assumptions help us make sense of complexity. After all, their craft is to interpret that seemingly boundless universe of facts we call 'the historical record'. An old school of thought saw this craft as the simple extraction of the facts, and in turn the truth, from available historical evidence. Real historians let the facts speak to them, it was argued, they don't impose themselves on the facts. Such views have long been criticized. 'It used to be said', the renowned historian and international relations scholar E. H. Carr wrote in his classic work *What is History?*, 'that facts speak for themselves. This is, of course, untrue. The facts speak only when the historian calls on them: it is he who decides which facts to give the floor, and in what order or context.' More recently, Quentin Skinner, one of the most influential historians of recent decades, has made a similar point. He uses the example of an English stately home, Chatsworth House. The facts about such a building are almost limitless, from the number of bricks to the ages of its many generations of servants. Which facts should the historian highlight? What if she made things more manageable by concentrating only on particular kinds of facts, for instance relating to works of art? While this seems like a good solution, all it does is highlight the importance of a historian's pre-existing assumptions: this time about what constitutes art. Does the art of Chatsworth House include the furniture, and if not, why not? Both Carr and Skinner are pointing to the same truth: that it is the things historians bring to their inquiries—the questions they ask, the concepts they employ, and the assumptions they make about what matters—that determine what counts as a fact and which facts make the stage. History, the distinguished British philosopher Michael Oakeshott wrote, 'is "made" by nobody save the historian: to write history is the only way of making it'.

Within the study of international relations, calls for robust empirical research instead of irrelevant theorizing are common. Yet for all of the reasons stated above, one can decry or fear theory but not escape it. Not even the greatest devotee of facts can study international relations without concepts—power, interests, sovereignty, the state, for example—and every one of these is an assumption that helps us makes sense of complexity. This is clearest in conceptual disagreements. Some assume that power is something individual actors possess, while others see it as a quality of particular kinds of relationships: between masters and slaves, for example. Still further, some think that power exists only when actors can successfully realize their goals: when A can get B to do what A wants, for example. But others insist that actors are powerful simply if they have disproportionate material capabilities, regardless of whether they wield them successfully to achieve desired ends. These contrasting assumptions about power lead scholars to read international relations differently, privileging some facts over others.

I have suggested that theories are nothing more than organized assumptions that enable us to make sense of complexity. The 'organized' part of this is important, as the assumptions we use to make sense of the world are not islands. When invited to a friend's place for dinner, my assumptions about what dinner entails, how to behave, and when to arrive and depart are all related. And to navigate this social space successfully, they will need to fit together coherently. Moreover, some assumptions are more fundamental than others. Everything rests, for example, on my assumptions about our friendship, as this will affect my assumptions about the nature of our dinner. Both will shape my assumptions about appropriate behaviour, which will also be affected by my understanding of prevailing social norms: does one bring a gift, are dinners formal affairs, which cutlery should I use with which course, is it okay to swear? In sum, in navigating this social occasion, I will weave my assumptions into a rudimentary, and probably subconscious, theory. Scientific theories—natural and social—are, of course, far more deliberate and systematic. But they consist, nonetheless, of nested assumptions, which we are expected to order in a logical and coherent fashion. Again, some of these assumptions are more fundamental than others. For example, as we will in the 'Six theories' section, some theories of international relations—like constructivism, the English School, and feminism—hold that international norms shape actors' identities and interests, and in turn their behaviour. These depend, however, on deeper assumptions—which we call 'ontological'—about the things that hold human social relations together: in this case, shared ideas, beliefs, and values.

Six theories

If there is a central message to the preceding discussion, it is this: embrace your inner theorist, and see the theorist in everyone. Since theorizing is inescapable—if we do it all the time in our daily lives, and if theoretical assumptions inform and structure all attempts to make sense of international relations—it is better to do it consciously and systematically than unreflectively. Reflecting on the assumptions we make about what matters in the world, considering how contrasting assumptions might lead us to read that world differently, and understanding how our arguments reflect underlying theoretical commitments all make us clearer and stronger students of international relations. It is not just about our own thinking, though: it is about how we engage and interpret the thought of others. It encourages us to read below the surface, to read for authors' central arguments, and to excavate the assumptions undergirding these arguments. This not only sharpens our critical eyes, and enables arguments to be compared and contrasted more systematically, it is also essential to respectful reading; to acknowledging how different arguments about international relations often reflect different starting assumptions, and while we might disagree with these, they remain assumptions, just like our own.

The rest of this chapter discusses six prominent theoretical perspectives on international relations. Theories of international relations are often differentiated into different kinds. The most common distinctions are between analytical and ethical theories and between mainstream and critical theories. In what follows I avoid such distinctions. While not without value, they can obscure much that this interesting about our most prominent theories. For example, I have written at length about how supposedly analytical theories, like realism, depend on ethical assumptions, and how purportedly ethical theories, concerning global distributive justice for example, rely on analytical assumptions. There is much to be gained, therefore, by reading against the grain of these common categorizations. I am interested, in particular, in what they might have in common. When I was a PhD student, I sat an exam for a course that stressed the differences between contending theories of international political economy. To my great shock, it asked me to write an essay on the similarities between these theories: on the things that bridged the divides I'd crammed so thoroughly. In what follows, I take a similar approach, reading key theories in terms of what they share: in particular, a common concern with the global organization of political authority.

The central proposition of *realist* thought is that international relations is a struggle for power. But there are different realist explanations for this struggle. Some, like Hans Morgenthau, attribute it to human nature, to the inherent human drive to dominate. Within states, they argue, where there is law, police, and courts, this drive is disciplined and contained. In such a world, civilization is possible. Between states, however, where there is no enforceable law, the drive to dominate goes unchecked, resulting in constant instability and recurrent violence. Other realists reject these views, holding that human nature is impossible to define (there are humanitarians and Nazis), and is thus a poor assumption on which to build an account of international relations. A more robust starting point, 'neo' or 'structural' realists like Kenneth Waltz argue, concerns the structure of the international system. The key feature of this structure is the absence of a central authority: there is no world government. In such an 'anarchic' system, all states—good and bad—have a fundamental interest in survival, the prerequisite for all other goals and objectives. But where there is no central authority—no institution to protect you when the going gets tough—states have to help themselves, and they do this by building their relative power, particularly military power. This generates a persistent 'security dilemma', however. When a state increases its military capabilities, other states, unclear about its motives, will hedge their bets by bolstering their own capabilities, fuelling arms racing and endless struggles for power. In both strands of realist thought, the only way to contain such struggles is through the balancing of power between states, where an equilibrium of capabilities instils caution and thus stability (the only form of peace realists entertain).

Given these views, how can realists be centrally concerned with the global organization of political authority? Political authority is *legitimate* power, and realists emphasize struggles for *material* power. Realists spend a lot of time thinking about the conditions needed to sustain ordered relations between states, and it is here that political authority enters their arguments. A minority of realists are thorough-going materialists, and see international order as a simple product of a balance of military and economic power. More commonly, realists think order also requires rules that enable states to coexist and cooperate. Of course, being realists such rules have to flow from, and be sustained by, the prevailing balance of power. A central theme of realist thought is that some balances of power are more conducive than others to the development and success of such rules, with hegemony—the leadership of a dominant state—often considered essential. A long tradition of realist 'hegemonic stability theory' holds that the rules needed to sustain order require the sponsorship and policing of a dominant state, like Britain in the 19th century or the US after 1945. Because of this, periods of hegemony are considered stable, but hegemonic transitions, when great powers struggle for primacy, are thought to bring instability and often war.

The crucial point in all of this is that hegemony is not just material dominance, it is a form of political authority. This is evident in two areas. First, hegemons are leaders, and they are recognized as such by other states. Realists have long acknowledged that legitimacy is essential to a hegemon's power, while insisting at the same time that a hegemon's disproportionate material capabilities greatly enhance its ability to cultivate such legitimacy. Second, the rules a hegemon sponsors have to be negotiated, not imposed. A hegemon's material might is essential to policing the rules, but realists commonly see the emergence of rules as the product of a grand bargain, in which the hegemon provides security and stability in return for the compliance of other states.

Liberalism is a general political theory translated to international relations. Where realists treat groups—particularly states—as primary, liberals start with individuals. They argue that legitimate states (invariably democracies) are built on a social contact with the individuals they rule, and such states exist solely to advance the interests and protect the rights of their citizens. Law is legitimate only if it is authored by those subject to it, or their representatives, and it must apply equally to all in all like cases. These ideas are translated to the international realm in three ways. Liberals follow the great philosopher, Immanuel Kant, in arguing, first, that democracies are more peaceful than autocracies, as citizens, who bear the greater costs of war, are more risk averse than monarchs and dictators (unless confronted by an easily demonized foe). Spreading democracy is thus considered essential to peace. Liberals also believe that their domestic principles of governance can be applied to the international arena. These include the rule of law, the notion that legal subjects are the only legitimate authors of that law, and that sovereign rights are conditional on the protection of individual rights. Liberals are thus generally strong supporters of international law, the collective negotiation of rules and norms, and the international protection of human rights. Finally, because liberals believe in the pacifying effects of commerce—in the ability of unfettered trade to produce shared interests—they are commonly vigorous advocates of international free trade. States who trade together without tariff barriers receive market determined fair prices for their goods, and become bound in webs of interdependence, which, in turn, raise the costs of conflict.

That liberalism is centrally concerned with the global organization of political authority is readily apparent. Concern with legitimate power permeates liberal international theory. Legitimate states are those based on popular sovereignty, and the proliferation and leadership of such states is considered essential to peace. Prominent liberals, such as Robert Keohane, also believe that it is rational and right for states to invest authority in international institutions (such as the UN, the WTO, and the Paris Agreement on Climate Change), as these enable states to coexist and cooperate. Finally, liberals share the realist interest in hegemony, especially liberal hegemony. While most states are interested in minimizing conflict and fostering cooperation, and liberal states favour institutional means to these ends, many argue that a liberal hegemon—like Britain or the US—is needed to seed a liberal international order, to sponsor the construction of an institutional architecture that secures the rule of law, free trade, and the protection of human rights. The leading liberal scholar of international relations, John Ikenberry, argues that this is precisely what the US did after 1945. It led to the construction of a 'liberal hegemonic order', one characterized by both commonly agreed upon institutional rules and practices and the widely accepted leadership of the US, first on the Western side of the Cold War and then globally.

Constructivists—as their name suggests—emphasize the socially constructed nature of international relations. They hold that humans only know the world around them through the social meanings they use to interpret that world, through the shared ideas and values that render things intelligible and assessable. Indigenous Australians and settler colonists, for example, occupy the same physical landscape, but they generally understand this environment very differently. The former see it as a spiritual realm, in which culture and land are deeply entwined; the latter commonly see it as a commodity, something that can be owned, priced, and exchanged. Leading constructivists, like Alexander Wendt, do not deny the existence of a 'real world', but they insist our knowledge of that world is mediated by frameworks of ideas, cultural symbols, and social discourses and practices.

In international relations, constructivism is characterized by three core propositions. First, while realists emphasize the importance of material power, constructivists think systems of ideas are equally important. For example, to the north of the US lies Canada, a rich middle power with significant military capacities, and to the south lies Cuba, a tiny impoverished developing state. Yet the US has long seen Cuba as a dire enemy. The material distribution of resources can't explain this: only the different meanings the US attaches to Canada and Cuba can. Second, constructivists argue that actors' interests, whether they be individuals or states, are shaped by their identities, by their senses of who they are and their understandings of how others see them. The US pursued a catalogue of interests after WWII, but these were not the interests Nazi Germany would have pursued: they reflect the US's identity as a liberal polity, an identity rooted in its national history and recognized and encouraged internationally. Finally, while constructivists emphasize the importance of social structures—shared ideas and practices—they insist that these are always the product of human beliefs and actions, which means that change is possible. Until the 20th century, for example, conquest was a core sovereign right, but today it is a violation of the cardinal principle of non-intervention.

Constructivist theorizing has focused on two broad issues, both directly related to the global organization of political authority. The first concerns the emergence and possible transformation of today's global system of sovereign states. At a time when most scholars took a world organized into sovereign states as a given, constructivists probed how it emerged in the first place, seeking insights into long-term dynamics of change. Not surprisingly, they have emphasized shifting ideas and beliefs. In one prominent line of argument, for example, John Ruggie contends that modern territorial sovereignty (see Chapter 2) could not emerge in Europe until medieval ideas of property rights—which saw them as non-exclusive 'use' rights—were replaced by the modern idea of exclusive property rights. This revolution allowed monarchs to claim supreme authority within their sovereign territories and exclude the claims of those outside. A second strand of constructivist theorizing has focused on the development of international norms, particularly in the areas of arms control, human rights, the environment, and regional governance. Norms are commonly defined as shared expectations of behaviour, and for leading constructivists, like Martha Finnemore and Audie Klotz, they do two things: they regulate what actors do, and, more deeply, they shape actors' identities. As we shall see in Chapter 6, international human rights norms codify the inalienable rights of individuals and the obligations states have to promote and protect these, and they provide a reference point against which states craft their identities. For example, Australian politicians frequently extol Australia as 'a gold star human rights state'. Just as the development of modern sovereignty parcelled political authority into territorially demarcated political units, the development of international norms establishes politically authoritative standards beyond the state. Moreover, for constructivists the two are deeply interconnected, as human rights norms seek to delineate the scope of legitimate sovereign authority.

The *English School* has much in common with constructivism, but it is best introduced via a comparison with realism. As we saw, realists stress the anarchic nature of the international system, its lack of a central authority. This alone, many of them argue, drives the incessant struggle for power. The English School is more sanguine, however. Even in the absence of a central authority, states can develop complex social relations: an 'anarchical society', as its key theorist Hedley Bull famously put it. Such a society exists, he argued,

> when a group of states, conscious of certain common interests and common values, form a society in the sense that they conceive themselves bound by a common set of rules in their relations with one another, and share in the working of common institutions.

At the very least, all states have interests in physical security, the stability of territorial property rights, and that promises, such as treaty commitments, will be kept. This leads them, the English School contends, to agree on shared rules (like the mutual recognition of sovereignty, the principles of non-intervention and self-determination, and limits on the use of force) and to construct institutions to uphold these rules (principally, diplomacy, international law, management by great powers, the coordinated balancing of power, and even war). The English School has focused considerable attention on how a nascent society of states emerged in Europe in the 15th century and gradually 'expanded' to encompass the globe, eventually resulting in today's global international society. There is also an intense debate between 'pluralists', who think that international society can only survive if cardinal principles like sovereignty and non-intervention are strictly observed, and 'solidarists' who hold that this society will fail (morally and practically) if these principles are not compromised in the name of human justice. These latter scholars were at the forefront of calls for humanitarian intervention in the 1990s, and have been leading proponents of the international doctrine of the 'Responsibility to Protect' (R2P), which holds sovereign states have a responsibility to protect their peoples, and when they fail to do this, the international community has a responsibility to step in.

In a sense, the English School's entire focus has been on the nature, history, and significance of a single configuration of political authority: European, then global, international society. This is explicitly not an arrangement of material power—an 'international system' in the School's parlance—it is a configuration of legitimate power. For its member states, international society, with its rules and institutions, is itself considered legitimate: it is their construction, sustained by their routinized practices. It is a configuration of political authority in a deeper sense, though. For realists, sovereign states exist so long as they can defend themselves, either on their own or with the aid of powerful allies. But for theorists of the English School it is international society that ordains states with sovereign rights: sovereignty is a status that has to be recognized by others. We see this in Western states' long denial of sovereign recognition to colonized peoples in the non-Western world (discussed further in Chapter 6), but also in the subsequent survival of materially weak but internationally recognized post-colonial states in the Global South (discussed in Chapter 2). Essential to both cases is the society of states' recognition of sovereign rights, or lack thereof.

Like realists, feminists are centrally concerned with power and security, and like liberalism, *feminism* is a general theoretical perspective translated to international relations. That translation has taken many forms, but feminist perspectives coalesce around several core ideas and commitments. Where realists focus on power differentials between sovereign states, especially between great powers, feminists concentrate on differences of power between genders, male over female. As pioneering feminist, Cynthia Enloe, has documented, men monopolize high office in most states, dominate the world's diplomatic corps, control the world's militaries, own most of the world's land but do a minority of agricultural labour, earn consistently higher wages than women, and more. Second, feminists argue that these are not just material differences, but are sustained by dominant systems of knowledge. What counts as valid knowledge, the concepts and theories we use to comprehend and order the world, the narratives we tell about our societies' histories and achievements, and acceptable modes of argument: all work to sustain gendered hierarchies of power, and license or obscure their consequences. For example, the world's militaries aren't just dominated by men, this is justified by deeply entrenched social conceptions of masculinity and femininity, about who can fight and who can't, conceptions woven into narratives of nationhood. Third, all of this has a profound effect on security. Gender hierarchies lie behind the epidemics of domestic violence that plague most national societies, and also behind the sexual violence that commonly attends civil and interstate wars. Moreover, feminists argue that male dominance of national decision-making, diplomatic processes, and military institutions increases the likelihood of war, escalating conflicts while foreclosing opportunities for cooperation. Feminist international theorists seek not only to understand the workings of gender in world politics, but also to critique and reformulate the assumptions that undergird international theory.

Like the other theories, feminism is centrally concerned with the global organization of political authority. But where all other theories treat political authority and its distribution as gender neutral, feminists stress its masculinist nature and gendered consequences. A good way to illustrate this is to return to the Lorenzetti fresco discussed in Chapter 1. There I used the fresco to explain political authority as rightful or legitimate power, but it illustrates equally well the gendered nature of such power. The legitimate ruler is male, bearing a sword and a shield (classic masculine symbols of power), and all of the citizens are male. Women feature prominently, but principally as civic virtues: justice, magnanimity, peace, etc. Lorenzetti's message is clear. Political authority is a masculine institution—and political agents are men. Women appear, as they have throughout history and in many cultures, as the symbolic moral guardians of authority, but not authorities. For feminist international theorists, this has been a defining feature of all global organizations of political authority. From hegemony and empire to international society, all are configurations of legitimate power, but all involve the privileging of male control through masculinized (and feminized) symbols, narratives, and practices. Feminist scholars, such Enloe, Jacquie True, Ann Tickner, and Laura Sjoberg, seek not only to understand the workings of these gendered structures of political authority, but to reject claims of social progress that are blind to gender hierarchies and sexual discrimination and violence.

I argued in Chapter 2 that what makes today's global system of sovereign states so fascinating is its novelty, the fact that it has existed for fifty years at best. Before that political authority was organized on the basis of empires, most connected to a small core of Western sovereign states. An inescapable implication of this is that we live in the shadow of empire, a shadow that profoundly affects the day-to-day play of international relations, the functioning of the world economy, continued patterns of inequality and exclusion, and racial and cultural narratives and identifications in former colonies and imperial heartlands. No body of theorizing confronts this reality more directly than *post-colonialism*. 'Domination and inequalities of power and wealth are perennial facts of human society', the pioneering post-colonial scholar Edward Said writes. 'But in today's global setting they are also interpretable as having something to do with imperialism, its history, its new forms.' It was imperialism that produced the legal distinctions between civilized, barbarian, and savage peoples, and it was the shadow of imperialism that translated these into the categories of first, second, and third worlds; and, later, developed and developing worlds. The material consequences of these hierarchical distinctions are readily apparent, and post-colonial scholars focus on critiquing and overturning the knowledge and practices that sustain them. A prominent strand of this work seeks to decentre the West by rereading the history and lived experience of imperialism from the perspective of the colonized. Another strand, elaborated in a recent volume by Alexander Anievas, Nivi Manchanda, and Robbie Shilliam, looks beyond the ideas and practices of formal empire to highlight the existence and consequences of a long-standing global 'colour line'. Distinctions between white and black, and the persistent hierarchizing of the former over the latter, run through and undergird almost all global axes of inequality: from continued racial inequities and violence in settler societies to the maldistribution of global wealth.

As will be clear, post-colonial theorists view the global organization of political authority through the lenses of imperialism, racial and cultural hierarchies, and their continued manifestations and consequences. Like the English School, post-colonialism stands out for its attention to the epochal transformation from a world of empires to a world of sovereign states, but it rejects as nonsense exaggerated claims like Robert Jackson's that as international society evolved 'it became blind to distinctions of race and culture and ideology, as well as religion and gender'. Precisely the opposite is true, they argue. Indeed, naïve assumptions that the end of empire saw a hierarchical world replaced by a world of sovereign equality obscure the persistence of racial hierarchies, rendering the language of formal or legal equality largely meaningless. And while a new wave of scholarship in international relations is challenging the old assumption that anarchy (the lack of a central authority) is the opposite to hierarchy, and arguing that very real hierarchies characterize today's anarchic system, post-colonial scholars go further, insisting that many of these hierarchies are racially inflected and have their origins in the colonial era. Finally, while many scholars applaud how international human rights norms limit or qualify the sovereign rights of states, post-colonial theorists highlight how the category of 'human' has only recently been considered universal, with those on the black side of the colour line long denied recognition as rights-bearing humans. They also highlight how human rights can be used as a legitimating ideology to justify intervention by powerful Western states.

Mix, match, and borrow

I have surveyed these theories to acquaint readers with several prominent theoretical perspectives on international relations, sketching their underlying assumptions and showing their distinctive takes on the global organization of political authority. Note, though, that no single theory can answer all of the many questions we can ask about international relations. And anyone who thinks their preferred theory can do this will quickly succumb to what I call 'Cinderella syndrome': the squeezing of an oversized world into a finely crafted yet ill-fitting theoretical slipper. A far better approach is to start with a fascinating question about international relations and then think openly about which existing theories, or new theoretical innovations, can best address this question. Often this means being eclectic, as mixing and matching ideas from different theories often provides the best purchase on a question. More than this, great insights frequently come from drawing on theoretical perspectives honed in other fields. Indeed, one of the great strengths of international relations as a field of study—something that has kept it vibrant and dynamic—has been its openness to ideas from fields like anthropology, economics, law, history, and sociology.

Chapter 4
War

Wars are currently tearing apart Afghanistan, Iraq, Libya, Sudan, Syria, and Yemen, to name only the most prominent cases. And while these conflicts are often described as 'civil wars'—wars between rival groups within states—external powers, such as Iran, Russia, Saudi Arabia, Turkey, and the US, are deeply implicated in them. Meanwhile, the global war on terror continues, in a seemingly endless attempt to suppress new forms of transnational non-state violence. Old-style interstate wars, where the armed forces of sovereign states battle for territorial control, have become far less common. But every day fears mount that escalating tensions between Iran and the US, India and Pakistan, the Ukraine and Russia, and in the South China Sea could see the return of war 'in the strict sense', as Hedley Bull termed it.

Some would cite all of this as evidence that international relations is not about the global organization of political authority, as argued here, but about struggles for material power, often violent. For them, Thucydides' famous *History of the Peloponnesian War* (fought between Athens and Sparta and their allies between 431 and 404 BC) captures the essence of international relations, where conquering Athenian generals tell the Melian people that 'the strong do what they have the power to do and the weak accept what they have to accept', and then proceed to kill all of the men and sell the women and children into slavery.

On closer inspection, however, war appears inextricably connected to the organization of political authority. War has played a key role, first of all, in constructing and sustaining systems of political authority. It was central to the emergence of sovereign states in Europe, for example, and the international community has routinely used war to secure the existing system of states (the war against ISIL being the most recent example). War-making has also been a prime *marker* of political authority. As the great sociologist Max Weber observed, a distinguishing feature of the sovereign state is its monopoly on the legitimate use of violence, a quality denied by definition to other actors. Finally, war has been the principal object of authoritative control in international relations. Establishing any kind of order between states requires, first and foremost, the subjection of warfare to agreed rules, about who has the legitimate authority to wage war, when it can be used legitimately, what kinds of violence are acceptable, and when they can be rightfully used.

Contrary to simplistic accounts, it is the connection between political authority and war that ultimately concerned Thucydides. His central theme in the *History* is the decline of Athenian hegemony, understood as legitimate power or authority. In reply to the Athenian declaration of 'might is right', the Melians warn that the Athenians

> should not destroy a principle that is to the general good of all men—namely, that in the case of all who fall into danger there should be such a thing as fair play and just dealing.... And this is a principle which affects you as much as anybody, since your own fall would be visited by the most terrible vengeance and would be an example to the world.

Thucydides hammers home the significance of these words in the final act of the *History*, the failed Athenian invasion of Sicily, where the Athenians 'were utterly and entirely defeated; their sufferings were on an enormous scale'.

This chapter explores the connections between war and the organization of political authority: how war shapes such organization, serves as its marker, and is itself the object of authoritative control. Together, these connections have profoundly affected the global organization of political authority, and vice versa. Before proceeding, a word is needed on my conception of war, as organized violence. In international relations, such violence has taken several key forms, and before concluding I consider how the balance between these has changed over time.

War as organized violence

In his classic work, *The Anarchical Society*, Hedley Bull argued that 'war in the strict sense' is 'international or interstate war, organized violence waged by sovereign states'. Examples of such wars are numerous: the 1803–15 Napoleonic wars, the 1851–2 Platine War in Latin America, the 1870 Franco-Prussian War, WWI, the 1931 Manchurian War, WWII, the 1965 India–Pakistan War, the 1973 Yom Kippur War, the 1990–1 Persian Gulf War, the 2003 Iraq War, and the list goes on. Countless lives have been lost in these and other interstate wars, and they have had a profound effect on the nature of politics and society. Yet our day-to-day use of the term 'war' departs widely from 'the strict sense'. We describe civil conflicts as 'wars', conflicts between states and transnational terrorists as 'wars', clashes between rival empires as 'wars', and violent confrontations between colonial powers and indigenous peoples as 'wars'.

Some might argue that this expansive use of the term war is sloppy talk, betraying sloppy thinking. Yet we are drawn to this usage for two compelling reasons. First, all of the above examples—strict and non-strict—involve organized, purposive violence. Quite rightly, our intuitions tell us that the frontier war white settlers waged against Australia's indigenous peoples, the 1899–1902 Boer War, and the 1980–8 Iran–Iraq War are different manifestations of war, not war in one case and something else in the others. Second, if we define war narrowly, as war between sovereign states, and apply this consistently, then the concept has limited analytical reach. To be sure, it accommodates many big and important conflicts. But as argued in Chapters 1 and 2, a world organized into sovereign states is a very recent development, and many violent, politically consequential conflicts have been between other kinds of actors. The Greco-Persian Wars (499–449 BC), the Roman conquest of Britain (beginning in 43 AD), the Wars of Spanish Succession (1701–14), and the Opium Wars (1839–42 and 1856–60): all involved actors other than sovereign states. Thinking beyond 'war in the strict sense' brings such conflicts into view, and enables us to think more broadly about the relationship between war and the shifting organization of political authority.

I thus follow the distinguished strategic analyst Lawrence Freedman in defining war as purposive, organized violence. War is 'purposive' violence because it is not random: it always serves certain ends. These ends can vary greatly. War, as organized violence, has been used to establish primacy or prestige, seize territory, overturn a regime, remake an international order, protect compatriots, crush domestic dissent, sow disorder and insecurity, eradicate or humiliate peoples, rape and pillage, fuel nationalism, reinforce social hierarchies, and it has been used to counter any or all of these. The key point, as Freedman explains, is that '[r]andom acts of violence or conflicts that are conducted without violence do not count as wars'. War is 'organized' violence, first, because it is crafted to achieve given purposes, and second, because it is collective: it involves social collaboration and coordination. Violence by lone individuals might be planned and carefully executed, but it lacks the collective element characteristic of war.

Historically, the global organization of political authority has been shaped by four main kinds of purposive, organized violence. The first is *wars of constitution*, where violence is used to remake the large-scale organization of political authority. The Wars of Religion that preceded the famous 1648 Peace of Westphalia are a case in point, as they played a key role in the demise of European heteronomy (see Chapter 2) and the emergence of a nascent system of sovereign states. The second kind is *wars of position*, where established units of political authority struggle for control or survival. These are the wars where city-states, empires, or sovereign states have used military force to expand or secure their rule. The Peloponnesian War between Athens and Sparta, the conflicts of China's Warring States era (475–221 BC), the Crimean War (1853–6), the two World Wars, and the Iran–Iraq War (1980–8) are all examples of this. The third kind is *wars of state-making*. These include the violence political elites have used to assert their control over rival elites or their own peoples. The 1965–6 killing of an estimated one million communists in Indonesia is one example, as are the Armenian, Nazi, and Rwandan genocides. Wars of state-making can also include revolutionary violence, aimed at ousting governments and transforming forms of political rule. Key examples include the violence of the French, Russian, and Chinese revolutions. The final kind of violence is *terrorism*, where violence is used by clandestine groups to force policy or institutional change or exacerbate social and political contradictions to undermine existing systems of social, economic, or political organization. The violence of ISIL, and that of white nationalist extremists (such as the terrorist attack on a Christchurch, New Zealand, mosque in March 2019), are prime contemporary examples.

Constructing and sustaining political authority

Realists have long argued that war plays a key role in the construction, maintenance, and exercise of political power, and in shaping and reshaping the distribution of power in an international system. Think only of the devastating violence of WWI, and few would deny war's capacity to tear apart old configurations of power and forge new ones. Yet war does more than simply redistribute material power, giving, for example, Britain, France, and the US more, and Germany and Turkey less. It also reorders and cements political authority. War helped create sovereign states, but war-making required rulers to strike bargains with their societies in order to legitimate their power and the state itself. Major wars rip apart international orders, but when wars end, victorious powers go to great lengths to construct a new order, defining which kinds of polities are legitimate and what are the bounds of legitimate political action. And once established, war is often a tool for the maintenance of an international order, for policing its rules and practices.

Eminent sociologist and political scientist Charles Tilly famously argued that 'war makes states'. His argument was more sophisticated, though, than the simple notion that war-fighting prowess is a necessary and sufficient condition for the emergence of sovereign states. Looking at the emergence of states in Europe, he argued that two kinds of warfare enabled early modern rulers to secure their rule. The first was the wars they fought to repel external rivals, what we call here 'wars of position'. Equally important, though, were the 'state-making' wars rulers fought to suppress internal rivals. Together, these forms of violence enabled them to establish primacy within a given territory. Tilly's argument does not stop there, though. To wage these wars rulers needed money and resources, and to secure these they had to strike bargains with leading social groups (landowners, merchants, etc.). In return for taxes, they promised these groups security and political rights, the latter resulting in constitutional constraints on their authority and the development of institutions like early parliaments. Both of these served to legitimate the sovereign state, to establish it as a unit of political authority not just power. A good example is the history of the English state, where, from the 1215 Magna Carta onward, the monarch's capacity to raise taxes (and fight wars) was dependent on the will of an evolving parliament.

A second way that wars shape the organization of political authority is by throwing old arrangements into the air and then compelling new ways of organizing politics. Not all wars do this, but it is a recurrent feature of major wars, conflagrations that engulf whole international systems, like WWI and WWII. Such conflicts never destroy all traces of a past order, but they pose, in stark relief, far-reaching questions about the value of that order, and provide unique opportunities for organizing political life differently. Not surprisingly, the wars that have most preoccupied Western international relations scholars—the Wars of Religion, the Napoleonic Wars, and the two World Wars—have been followed by major peace conferences (Westphalia, the Congress of Vienna, Versailles, and San Francisco), the primary purpose of which has been to construct a new international political order that prevents a return to war. Framing these deliberations have always been beliefs about what caused the conflict, and these go well beyond who started it, to include ideas about the economic, social, and political conditions that germinated the conflict (religious divisions, imperial rivalry, arms racing, economic collapse, etc.). Efforts to construct a new international order invariably reflect compromises between the political interests of key actors and their favoured strategies to address sources of instability. Three questions dominate these negotiations, however: what will be the legitimate political units (monarchies, empires, nation-states, etc.); what, if any, limits should be placed on the legitimate use of force; and what institutions are needed to peacefully resolve conflicts? The Peace of Versailles, which concluded WWI, sought to address each of these. In Europe, the legitimate political units were to be ethnically-defined nation-states, while empires were to rule elsewhere. To prevent war, a new global organization was established, the League of Nations, and its members were required to submit all conflicts to international arbitration. Any conflicts not submitted were to be declared illegal and warring parties subjected to international sanctions. The tragic failure of these institutional solutions is carved deep into 20th-century history, but while the Peace of Versailles failed to prevent a collapse back into world war, it had a profound effect on the organization of political authority, not the least by replacing the German, Austro-Hungarian, and Ottoman empires with a host of new sovereign states.

In addition to helping to generate units of political authority like sovereign states, and providing an opportunity and imperative to refashion the political landscape, war has been a tool for policing historical arrangements of political authority. Hedley Bull, whose view of war we encountered earlier, identified five fundamental institutions that have been used to sustain order among sovereign states: diplomacy, international law, management by the great powers, the balancing of power, and last but not least, war itself. Students often struggle to comprehend war as an institution, but Bull meant two things by this. He saw war itself as a rule-governed activity: it is always structured by underlying norms, like gendered medieval codes of chivalry or today's bonds of brotherhood between soldiers, and by more formal rules, like the laws of war (which we return to below). What matters here, though, is that he also saw war as a socially accepted means of upholding the rules of international society. In a world where political authority is organized into independent sovereign states, basic principles, such as mutual respect for sovereignty, non-intervention, and self-determination, have to be defended. And historically war has been an important means of doing this. A textbook example is the 1990–1 Persian Gulf War. After Iraq invaded neighbouring Kuwait, in clear violation of the legal rule of non-intervention, the UN Security Council authorized, under the enforcement provisions of Chapter VII of the Charter, a US-led coalition of states 'to use all necessary means…to restore international peace and security in the area'. The coalition then launched a massive military operation, successfully expelling Iraqi forces from Kuwait but at the cost of an estimated 30,000 Iraqi lives (Figure 2). A less clear cut case is the 2011 humanitarian intervention in Libya, which was also sanctioned by the UN Security Council. For many

2. War to uphold the rules of international society: the 'Highway of Death', Iraq 1991.

this is an example of states rightfully upholding the new doctrine of the 'Responsibility to Protect'—under which the international community has a responsibility to prevent states committing mass atrocities—but for others it was a violation of the more fundamental rule of non-intervention (especially as the Security Council had authorized the protection of civilians not regime change). Both positions, however, accepted that war is a rule-governed practice and an important means for upholding the norms of international society. They just disagree about what these norms were, and which had priority.

War as a marker of political authority

As well as helping to construct and sustain forms of political authority, war-making has also become a jealously guarded badge of such authority, especially in today's world of sovereign states. As we saw above, Max Weber famously defined the sovereign state as a 'human community that (successfully) claims the monopoly of the legitimate use of physical force within a given territory'.

He intended this as a guide to analysis, a neat definition that would clarify what the state is. But he also pointed to an important political reality. Sovereign states are today the principal centres of political authority across the globe, and as part of defending this privileged status, they vigorously assert their monopoly over the legitimate use of violence. This is not a claim that they are the only entities that physically can or do use violence: pub brawlers, abusive spouses, rapists, murderers, and insurgents are violent too. Rather, it is a claim that states, and states alone, can use violence *legitimately*: to rightfully enforce the law, repel aggressors, uphold international law, and so on. As we shall see, this right is not unqualified: international rules and norms have evolved that limit when states can use violence legitimately. It remains the case, however, that among the privileged rights of sovereigns, the legitimate exercise of violence is primary.

The idea that states alone can and should have a monopoly on the legitimate use of violence is relatively new, however. As late as the 19th century, European states lacked the capacity to use force across their domains, especially in their empires. It was common, therefore, to acknowledge other actors' rights to use violence when it served the political interests of the state. In the 14th and 15th centuries, Italian city-states like Florence and Milan relied on mercenary *condottieri* to fight their incessant wars for regional supremacy. In 1584 England's Queen Elizabeth I authorized the privateer Sir Walter Raleigh to sail to the Americas 'to discover, search, finde out, and view such remote, heathen and barbarous lands, countries and territories', to colonize lands he deemed valuable, and to wage war to 'encounter and expulse, repell and resist' all those who obstructed him. And until the 1857–8 Sepoy Rebellion, the British Empire in India was governed not by the state, but by the privately owned British East India Company. It was the Company's army that enforced imperial rule, an army that by the start of the 19th century is said to have been twice the size of the official British army. The Sultan of Mysore so hated the Company that he had made an automated tiger mauling a

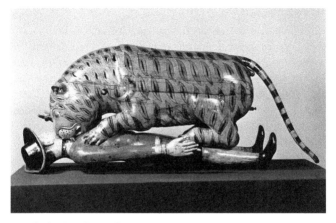

3. *Tipu's Tiger*: **late 18th century.**

European man, the former symbolizing himself, the latter the
Company (see Figure 3).

In the 20th century, the collapse of Europe's empires and the
global spread of sovereign states was accompanied by heightened
efforts to secure the state's monopoly on the legitimate use of
force. Two examples illustrate this. First, where anti-colonial
struggles turned violent, as they did in Algeria for example,
colonial powers commonly sought to delegitimize the violence of
independence fighters, with France casting the Algerians as
'terrorists'. Attempts were later made to define the violence of
self-determination struggles as lawful self-defence against colonial
rule, and, conversely, to define the use of force by imperial powers
against such struggles as illegitimate. Yet when decolonization had
run its course, newly independent post-colonial states vigorously
asserted their monopoly over the legitimate use of force, casting
insurgent, revolutionary, or secessionist violence within their
newly independent states as criminal. Second, the laws of war
(discussed below) were refined to define only the soldiers of
sovereign states as legal combatants. For example, the 1977

First Additional Protocol to the Geneva Conventions (the key locus of international law relating to humanitarian treatment in war) defines mercenaries as unlawful combatants, and thus not entitled to the protections accorded to prisoners of war. This was followed in 2001 by the International Convention against the Recruitment, Use, Financing and Training of Mercenaries, which seeks to ban the use of mercenaries altogether. Many leading states, such as the US, have not signed this convention, fearing that it will constrain their widespread use of what are known as Private Military Contractors. In other areas, however, these states have drawn tight boundaries around who constitute legal combatants. Since the attacks of 11 September 2001 the US has insisted that terrorists are unlawful combatants, not entitled to the normal protections of the laws of war.

War as the object of control

If war has been an engine for the construction and reconstruction of political authority, and if the right to wage war came to be a marker of the sovereign state's authority, it has also been a practice in dire need of control. Indeed, no way of organizing political authority—be that today's world of sovereign states, the world of empires that preceded it, or the heterogeneous political order of medieval Europe—can have any stability, let alone peace, unless organized violence is contained within socially accepted limits. Human societies have used all sorts of means to do this, from the development of norms governing male violence to the restriction of the use of force to authorized state agencies, such as the police or military. In modern international relations, however, three means have dominated: (1) establishing rules that limit when war can be waged legitimately (*jus ad bellum*), (2) codifying the kinds of violence that are permissible in war (*jus in bello*), and (3) giving international bodies the right to arbitrate conflicts, decide their legitimacy, authorize the use of force, and, most recently, prosecute those guilty of war crimes. Each one of these has reshaped the global organization of political authority.

Since the 19th century, a dramatic shift has occurred in the international legal rules governing when war could rightfully be waged. When European imperialism accelerated in the second half of the century—manifest most dramatically in the 'Scramble for Africa'—states enjoyed a legal right of conquest. In other words, according to European standards, if a state succeeded in establishing control over a territory and its people, it became the legitimate sovereign authority. Nowhere was this more clearly asserted than in Chapter VI of the General Act of the 1884–5 Berlin Conference on West Africa, where the imperial powers agreed that to secure their sovereignty over conquered territories they had to give each other formal notification and establish an effective administering authority. The calamitous implications of this largely unfettered right to wage war were exposed in stark relief by WWI. And in 1928 leading states signed the Kellogg–Briand Pact, in which they condemned 'recourse to war for the solution of international controversies, and renounce[d] it, as an instrument of national policy in their relations with one another'. This legal instrument was gravely insufficient to prevent the onset of WWII, barely a decade after the Pact was signed. The subsequent loss of an estimated seventy to eighty-five million lives only confirmed, however, the need to bring warfare under control. In 1945 the Charter of the newly created UN defined only two conditions in which the use of force was legal: in self-defence against an armed attack (Article 51), and as part of a Security Council approved action 'to maintain or restore international peace and security (Article 39). These rules have proven far more successful than the 1928 Pact and are now widely considered the definitive principles by which the legitimacy of war is judged. Debate has persisted, however, over when a conflict constitutes a threat to 'international peace and security', warranting Security Council action. For example, advocates of the doctrine of the 'Responsibility to Protect' hold that when all else fails the international community has a responsibility to intervene militarily to prevent mass atrocities, such as ethnic cleansing and genocide. Others reject such arguments, claiming that R2P stretches the notion of threats to international peace and security too far, and that humanitarian interventions violate the sovereign right to non-intervention.

Limiting *when* wars can be fought legitimately is but one step in constraining their harmful effects. Limiting *how* they can be fought is equally crucial. Even if wars can be limited to self-defence and the maintenance of international peace and security, it would be catastrophic if they were waged with chemical, biological, or nuclear weapons, or if victors routinely killed all of the defeated men and sold all of the women into slavery, as the Athenians did to the Melians. Since the late 19th century a second strand of the laws of war has sought to address this issue, focusing on three key areas. The first has involved banning the use of particular kinds of weapons. The Hague Convention of 1899 banned the use of poison, the dropping of explosives from balloons, the firing of projectiles with asphyxiating gases, and the use of expanding bullets. More recent developments include treaties banning biological weapons (1972), chemical weapons (1992), landmines (1997), cluster munitions (2008), and a new treaty that seeks to ban nuclear weapons (2017). There is also a major campaign under way to outlaw the use of lethal autonomous weapons systems (killer robots). The second area concerns the treatment of military combatants. Crucial here are the four Geneva Conventions of 1864, 1906, 1929, and 1949, as well as their three additional protocols of 1977 (the first two) and 2005 (the third). The final area addresses the targeting of non-combatants. Efforts to control such targeting date back to the first Geneva Convention of 1864, but the large-scale bombing of civilians during WWII spurred further action, resulting in the 1949 Geneva Convention. In recent years attempts have been made to tighten these prohibitions further, most notably with regard to the use of rape in war.

Limiting when war can be fought legitimately, and prohibiting certain ways of fighting wars, circumscribe the political authority of sovereign states, stating in clear legal terms that sovereign rights are not boundless. Attempts to contain war have gone beyond this, though, often involving the granting of authority to other actors and institutions. There is a long tradition, for example, of requiring conflicting parties to submit their disputes to third party arbitration. The Ancient Greek city-states practised this successfully for centuries, and one of the grievances Sparta and its allies had against Athens was its refusal to arbitrate their differences. Similarly, Article 12 of the 1919 Covenant of the League of Nations required member states to submit any disputes likely to lead to conflict 'to arbitration or judicial settlement or enquiry by the Council', and not to go to war until three months after a decision. Another example of how authority has been transferred to third parties concerns the actual decision to go to war. Recall that the UN Charter allows only two legitimate uses of force: self-defence and multilateral actions authorized by the UN Security Council to uphold international peace and security. In the second of these cases (evident in the 1990–1 Gulf War, discussed above), it is the UN Security Council that has the power to authorize war. A third area where authority has been invested in international bodies is the prosecution of crimes of aggression, war crimes, and crimes against humanity, such as genocide. After WWII ad hoc tribunals were established in Nuremberg and Tokyo to prosecute German and Japanese leaders, but it was not until after the end of the Cold War that a permanent international criminal court was established. In response to the atrocities of the Yugoslav wars (1991–2001) and the Rwanda genocide (1994), the UN Security Council established two ad hoc tribunals: the International Criminal Tribunal for the Former Yugoslavia (ICTY), and the International Criminal Tribunal for Rwanda (RCTR). There was a widespread view, however, that a permanent court was needed, and in 1998 states adopted the Rome Statute of the International Criminal Court (ICC). The Court came into operation in 2002, and, based in The Hague, it has the authority to hear cases involving alleged genocide, crimes against humanity, and war crimes; and the crime of aggression is likely to be added to this list. This granting of authority to the ICC has become increasingly controversial, however, with prominent African states leading criticisms that the Court's focus is on alleged crimes in non-Western developing countries and it has failed to address the purported crimes of Western nations, particularly the US.

Shifting forms of organized violence

Earlier I suggested that four main forms of organized violence have historically shaped the global organization of political authority: wars of constitution, wars of position, wars of state-making, and terrorism. Over the course of the past century, a dramatic shift has occurred in the relative frequency of these types of violence. To begin with, wars of position—the ones fought between states with armies, navies, and air forces—have become increasingly rare. Not only have they declined in absolute numbers, this has occurred at the very same time as the number of recognized sovereign states has quadrupled, from around fifty in 1945 to almost 200 today. So while the potential sources and sites of conflict should have increased, the number of traditional interstate wars has, in fact, plummeted. Similarly, wars of constitution, that seek to reshape the large-scale organization of political authority, are almost non-existent at the moment. The era of anti-colonial wars, which sought to replace empires with sovereign states, ended when post-1945 decolonization had run its course. The failed war by ISIL to found a new caliphate in the Middle East is perhaps the only recent example of such violence. Sadly, the trend for the other two kinds of violence runs in the opposite direction. Wars of state-making—where elites kill their own people, or insurgents or revolutionaries seek political change or control—continue to wreak havoc on societies. The conflicts in Afghanistan, Libya, Myanmar, South Sudan, and Syria all testify to this. Terrorism also remains a prominent form of global violence, and has now assumed novel transnational forms, enabled by the ongoing revolution in communications technology. Two things should be noted here, however. Although attacks on

Western countries receive most attention, most terrorism occurs in war torn societies of the Global South, such as the Central African Republic, the Democratic Republic of Congo, Sri Lanka, and Yemen (where there is a close connection between terrorism and wars of state-making). And while global terrorism has increased since the attacks of 11 September 2001, it has fluctuated in intensity and lethality, reflecting the fortunes of key terrorist groups such as ISIL, the evolution of prominent civil wars, and the effectiveness of national and international counterterrorism initiatives. These trends raise many fascinating questions, but two are of critical importance. What kind of international order—what way of organizing political authority globally—generates these patterns of violence? And how can we foster the aspects that have led to declines in wars of constitution and position while reducing the violence of state-making and terrorism? The field of international relations strives to answer such fundamentally important, yet profoundly difficult, questions.

Chapter 5
Economy

All social and political life takes place within economies. Life is enmeshed in ways of producing things, systems of exchange, class relations, and flows of money and capital. And it is entangled in, and shaped by, the forms of knowledge that render all of these intelligible and legitimate. International relations are no exception, and the impact of the global economy on international life is everywhere to be seen. The 2008 GFC undermined the global leadership of the US, challenged institutions of global governance, and set alarm bells ringing again about the destabilizing political effects of increasing economic inequality within and between societies. And as important forms of economic wealth and resources have shifted to the East, the sense has spread that international relations are at a crucial turning point: the end of the American century, and the beginning of the Asian.

The influence of economic processes, structures, and practices is nothing new. Debate persists about what caused the acceleration and intensification of European imperialism in the second half of the 19th century, evident in the 'Scramble for Africa', the Opium Wars in China, and Britain's assumption of direct rule in India. Few would deny altogether the influence of economic factors, however: especially the impact of Europe's industrial revolution, and the demand it generated for raw materials, new markets, and profitable investments. Old arguments that attributed this revolution to discrete features of European civilization— Protestantism, the decentralized system of sovereign states, the rise of commercial cities and classes, and sheer European genius—have been widely discredited, and Europe is now seen as the beneficiary of a prior age of globalization that originated in Asia and the Middle East. Between 500 and 1800 AD the economic powerhouses of the world lay in these regions, and global trade networks, especially emanating from China, facilitated the flow of ideas, institutions, and technologies westward, ultimately underpinning Europe's industrial take off and its new age of imperialism. What these differing explanations share, however, is a sense of the importance of economic forces and processes in shaping international relations.

Scholars differ on how economies affect international relations. At one extreme, there are those who stress the primacy of competition for political power and the secondary, supporting role of economics. In this view the desire for power is the driver, power flows from the barrel of a gun, and money is needed to buy guns. For example, Chapter 4 discussed the argument that war made states, that rulers had to wage war to suppress their rivals, and because they needed money to sustain such conflicts, they struck bargains with merchant classes, ultimately creating the institutions of what became modern states. At the other extreme, some scholars see international relations as a simple expression of underlying economic forces, attributing the contours of political power, the nature of political institutions, and the fundamental interests of political actors to the underlying dynamics and logic of capitalism. The eminent sociologist Immanuel Wallerstein famously argued, for example, that the capitalist world-economy divides the globe into three zones—the wealthy centre, poor periphery, and transitional semi-periphery—and that the existence, nature, and interests of sovereign states within these zones are determined by their position within the capitalist system.

Most scholars reject these extremes and seek more nuanced understandings of the relation between economic conditions and international relations. By focusing international relations on the global organization of political authority, this book suggests one such understanding. Economies are not self-generating or sustaining, their very nature, operation, and success *depends* on systems of political authority. As we shall see, money is itself a social institution, backed by political authority; market competition succumbs to inefficient and unfair monopolies without political regulation; and without political intervention, markets routinely fail to deliver desired social goods, from public health to environmental sustainability. The reverse, however, is also true: the legitimacy of political power, institutions, and practices depends, in significant measure, on the distribution of economic benefits and burdens: wealth, jobs, taxes, and more. Just as war-fighting, as well as efforts to constrain its uses and effects, have shaped the global organization of political authority, so too has the interaction between, and mutual dependence of, economies and legitimate political power.

This chapter explores this relationship. After considering in greater detail the connections between economies and political authority, it highlights three shifting global conditions that have, over the past century, affected this relationship: changes in the world economy, particularly in the nature of trade and the balance between trade and finance; revolutions in technology, from heavy industry to cyber; and shifts in the global distribution of economic resources from the West to the East. It then addresses the shifts in political authority that have shaped, and been shaped by, these changing global conditions, focusing in particular on the change from a world of empires to a global system of sovereign states, the rise and fall of hegemons, changes in the nature of international institutional regulation, and the development of different state–economy relations. The chapter concludes with a brief discussion of three major economic challenges facing the global organization of political authority: the rise of new economies and actors, inequality and social dislocation, and the accelerating global environmental crisis.

Economies and political authority

While dominant economic theories imagine a pure economy that is not structured by, and dependent upon, political authority, it is near impossible to identify such a thing in the real world. Even the most basic forms of exchange depend on social norms—shared ideas of rightful ownership and prohibitions on theft, for example—and although such norms are at times informal, most societies codify them in law, backed by legitimate political power. Money provides another example of the dependence of economies on political authority. It is so much a part of our daily lives that we can easily think of it as a natural, material thing. But money is a social institution, based on shared understandings that 100 yuan, rupees, euros, or US dollars have certain values, exchangeable for certain goods. Moreover, it is a social institution backed by states, which mint notes and coins, uphold them as legal tender, and intervene in markets to protect their value. This is why the oldest discovered coins through to the most recently minted bank notes bear (as Figure 4 shows) the imprints of emperors, monarchs, presidents, or national symbols (from eagles to kangaroos).

4. Queen Victoria on British East Africa Protectorate coin, 1898.

Another example concerns market competition, often seen as an entirely natural process. Yet one of the most compelling insights of Marxist theorists, most famously the Russian revolutionary Vladimir Lenin, is that capitalism tends toward monopolies, in which markets become dominated by ever fewer and more powerful companies (think of Amazon and Google today). Ensuring competition requires political intervention, and today most states have agencies and laws to prevent, and at times break up, monopolies. Finally, markets frequently fail to deliver desirable social outcomes, and political action is often required to shape or constrain economic forces to achieve particular ends. Markets in firearms are a good example. Unregulated, such markets lead to the proliferation of ever more dangerous weapons, resulting in escalated violence and increased fatalities (the experience of the US being a case in point).

The relationship between economies and political authority is not a one-way street, though: legitimate political power depends, in significant measure, on appropriate economic conditions and dynamics. Such power can rest on a range of non-economic factors, from ideas of divine right and charismatic leadership to electoral success and democratic accountability. Yet all political systems shape how economic benefits and burdens are distributed, and the nature of this distribution affects the legitimacy of political actors, institutions, and practices. How wealth, jobs, access to markets, the benefits of technology, and the knowledge needed to reap economic gains are distributed all bear on political legitimacy, as does the responsiveness of social and political institutions to demands for economic change. This is clearly apparent when states hold elections, when more often than not how political parties claim to manage the economy dominates debate. More dramatically, it is evident in the complete collapse of political systems in the wake of economic crises. The end of Germany's Weimar Republic in 1933 and the rise of Nazism is one example, and the fall of Indonesia's Suharto regime after the 1997 Asian financial crisis is another. Large-scale configurations of political authority, like empires, have also been shaken by flagging economic conditions. Some attribute the 19th-century decline of the Ottoman Empire to its failing economy and unresponsive political institutions. And it is often claimed that the current rise of populism (right and left wing) in many states is a product of the 2008 GFC and the longer-term effects of economic globalization on the distribution of jobs and wealth in many societies. Disenchantment with economic crisis and change has also spilled over borders, with populists now challenging the legitimacy of international institutions, from the EU to the WTO.

Shifting global conditions

Over the past century the relationship between the economy and the global organization of political authority has been shaped by three shifting, interrelated conditions: changes in the world economy, industrial and technological revolutions, and movements in the global distribution of economic resources, most recently from the West to the East. It is useful to consider each of these before turning to changes in the organization of political authority.

When considering long-term changes in the global economy, two modern periods of 'globalization' have been crucial, periods when economic interactions across borders and between societies increased and intensified. The first, which extended from the mid-19th century until the start of WWI, saw a dramatic expansion of global agricultural and manufacturing trade. Europe's industrial revolution, enabled by the spread of railways and improvements in shipping, and supported by British pressure on other states to lower tariffs (taxes) on imported goods, pushed the value of exported goods in 1913 to 13.9 per cent of world gross domestic product (GDP), the total of gross national incomes for every country in the world (see Ortiz-Ospina et al.). Two things are notable about this trade. Trade in agricultural goods dominated, amounting to 54 per cent of world merchandise

5. Mahatma Gandhi spinning.

exports in 1925 (see WTO, *World Trade Report 2013*). Moreover, this period saw a flood of European manufactured goods into the poorer, colonized parts of the world, thereby undermining the industrialization of these regions and establishing the long-term divide between the capital and manufacturing intensive West and the capital-poor agricultural economies of the Global South. In protest against this deindustrialization, Mahatma Gandhi, the revered Indian nationalist, famously championed the use of hand-woven Indian textiles and the boycotting of foreign-made cloth (see Figure 5).

The second period of globalization started in 1945 and continues today. The growth in the value of exports as a percentage of world GDP in this period eventually dwarfed that of earlier globalization. By 2008 it had peaked at 27 per cent, and while suffering a steep decline with the onset of the GFC, it had rebounded to 24 per cent of world GDP by 2014 (see Ortiz-Ospina et al.). As we will see below, this expansion of world trade was the product of very particular political conditions. It is not just the volume of trade that is important, however. The mix of things traded has changed just as dramatically. Where trade in agricultural goods dominated prior to WWII, by 2011 it had dropped to only 9 per cent of world merchandise exports, and manufactured goods had jumped to 65 per cent (see WTO, *World Trade Report 2013*). In addition to this, trade in services—travel, transport, business, education, communications, and financial and insurance services—has grown from 17 per cent of world trade to 23 per cent (see RBA, 'International Trade in Services'). The growth in financial services reflects the increasing importance of financial flows, transactions, and relations in the world economy that occurred prior to the 2008 crisis. According to the Organization for Economic Co-operation and Development (OECD), global cross-border inflows of capital grew from 5 per cent of world GDP in 1995 to 20 per cent in 2007. Before the GFC, the rise first of trade in manufactured goods, and then trade in services, along with the dominance of global finance, characterized the second period of globalization. Since the crisis, however, an entirely new phenomenon has emerged: digital globalization, the rapid spread of digital technologies, applications, and interactions (see McKinsey, *Digital Globalization*). Global flows of goods and finance have not been diminished by this development: rather, they have benefited from dramatic increases in flows of data and information. Indeed, it is argued that all such flows now have a digital component. The effects on the global economy are far-reaching. Most notably, while the digitalization of the global economy has spawned new corporate giants, like Apple, Facebook, and Google, it has also lowered the costs of 'going global', opening the door to new market participants.

This new turn in the global economy points to the importance of industrial and technological revolutions, the recurrence of which has been hastened by the competitive dynamics of capitalism. It is common to identify at least three such revolutions over the past two-and-a-half centuries, with a possible fourth now under way. The first took off in Britain in the mid-18th century, where steam power revolutionized manufacturing, first in textiles, and transformed transportation, enabling the rapid spread of railways and the acceleration of global shipping. The second revolution unfolded from around 1870 and involved the harnessing of electricity to enable the mass production of manufactured goods. Emblematic of this revolution is Henry Ford's famous introduction of a moving assembly line to manufacture cars for a mass market. So too, though, is the manufacture of heavy armaments (guns, tanks, warships, nuclear weapons) that enabled the destruction of WWI and WWII. The third revolution came in the late 1960s with the advent of digital computer technology.

The impact of this revolution is all around us: in how we construct and maintain our social networks, in our work places and practices, in our modes of entertainment, in the working of more traditional technologies, like cars, and in the nature and reach of government. Its essence, the influential social theorist Jeremy Rifkin argues, is the 'ability to reduce communications, visual, auditory, physical, and biological systems, to pure information that can be reorganized into vast interactive networks that operate much like complex ecosystems'. Some, like President of the World Economic Forum Klaus Schwab, argue that the world is in the midst of a fourth industrial revolution, one that takes the digital revolution to a qualitatively new level. The key feature of this revolution is 'a fusion of technologies that is blurring the lines between the physical, digital, and biological spheres'. Critics, like Rifkin, argue that this is simply an extension or elaboration of the third revolution. But proponents insist that radical technological innovations, such as nanotechnology, 3D printing, and high speed mobile computing networks, have not only produced a quantum leap in the speed and scale of digital interactions, but also blend cyber and physical systems, with profound implications for biological and social life.

While these transformations in the nature of the global economy were taking place, and as they were intersecting with industrial and technological changes, major shifts were occurring in the distribution of economic resources and capabilities between states and regions. It is important to recall at this point that while the last few decades have seen a shift in economic resources from the West to the East, prior to 1800 it was Asia and the Middle East that were the economic powerhouses, and it was globalization emanating from those regions that enabled Europe's industrial revolution. Zooming forward to the late 19th century onward, three key shifts stand out. The first is between the two Western hegemons: Britain and the US. In 1890 Britain, together with its imperial holdings in India, had the world's largest GDP, substantially larger than the US and China, the next two largest. (Note that all GDP figures are GDP by Purchasing Price Parity (PPP): see the Glossary.) By 1930, however, the GDP of the US was three times larger than those of China and Britain, and by 1980 neither of these countries ranked in the world's five largest economies. The second major shift has come since the 1990s, with the dramatic resurgence of China. By 2000 China had replaced Japan as the world's second largest economy, and in 2014 its GDP passed that of the US. The third shift concerns the dwindling economic dominance of the West in general. In 2018, of the world's ten largest economies, China was first, India third, Japan fourth, Russia sixth, Indonesia seventh, and Brazil eighth. A fourth, and final, shift merits attention. Since 1945 most economic exchanges have been between either wealthy developed countries, or between developed and developing countries. But since the 1990s economic interactions between countries of the Global South has grown markedly. For example, since 1996 trade between these states has grown at over 12 per cent each year, twice the growth of North–South trade. (Note, though, that these figures are based on trade and investment, but in the area of finance countries such as China have arguably become more dependent on US-dominated money markets.)

Changes in global political authority

None of these changes occurred in a political vacuum. At the most fundamental level, they were affected by the most significant systems change in international relations for five centuries: the transformation from a world of empires to a global system of independent sovereign states (see Chapter 2). They were also affected by US hegemony, which until recently gave Washington elevated political authority in the new sovereign order. They were enabled and shaped by developments in multilateral governance and regulation. And they were driven and conditioned by the different kinds of state–economy relations that emerged in different countries.

The post-1945 decolonization of Europe's empires involved a fundamental shift in the global distribution of legitimate political power. Empires were thoroughly delegitimized, and for the first time in world history sovereign states became the primary units of political authority. If we return to the maps in Chapter 2, the world shifted from Map 2 to a global version of Map 1. Some observers attribute this change to economic factors: to the parlous economic position of Europe's imperial powers after WWII, making empire unaffordable; and to the changing needs of capitalism, which no longer required formal empires to thrive. Yet, as Chapter 6 explains, powerful political forces drove the end of the empire, not the least being struggles for individual rights. Whatever its causes, though, the dramatic reconfiguration of political authority that attended decolonization had a major effect on the global economy.

For one thing, when European states were separated from their colonies, they dropped in world GDP rankings. At the moment of India's independence in 1947, for example, Britain was displaced by the Soviet Union as the world's second largest economy. Decolonization also had an immediate impact on the politics of international economic regulation. By the 1970s, post-colonial states were a majority in the UN, and for over a decade they used their numbers to campaign for a 'New International Economic Order' (NIEO), seeking to secure their economic as well as political independence. They sought international rules allowing them to regulate multinational corporations that operated unfettered within their borders, to nationalize foreign-owned property that persisted from the colonial era, to form associations to secure fair commodity prices (after the Organization of Petroleum Exporting Countries, OPEC, had used an export embargo in 1973–4 to force oil price increases), to gain technology transfers from advanced economies, and to protect their sovereignty over natural resources. The NIEO is generally thought to have failed, defeated by the concerted efforts of the US and the march of free market, deregulatory economics that swept the world during the 1980s (see below). Yet its political legacies are significant, evident in the persistence of economic development as an enduring international norm (ever present in international trade and environmental negotiations), in ongoing, if evolving, groupings of post-colonial states (such as the G77), and in the issues that continue to stall the Doha round of world trade negotiations (which we touch on below).

While decolonization removed old imperial hierarchies, the new world of legally equal sovereign states had its own hierarchies, the most significant of which was US hegemony. The US emerged from WWII the preeminent economic and military power. Yet hegemony is more than material primacy, it is a social status, a position of leadership, recognized by other states in the system, a position that gives the hegemon special rights but also responsibilities. Most commentators agree that the US enjoyed such a status on the Western side of the Cold War divide from 1945 until the early 1970s, and globally from the early 1990s until the GFC. And few question the crucial role that the US played in shaping the post-1945 economic order. As we will see, it led the design and establishment of the Bretton Woods financial and trading institutions, the US dollar formally underwrote their operation until the 1970s, and the US provided the lion's share of their budgets. As a consequence, the US wielded the greatest political influence over the operation of these institutions. It was long held that American hegemony ended in the early 1970s (for reasons explained below), but many see the immediate post-Cold War era as a 'unipolar moment', when the US again enjoyed hegemonic authority. The GFC brought this moment to an abrupt end, however, even if, as noted above, the US still wields considerable power in international money markets that depend on US Treasury Bonds.

A key feature of the post-1945 global organization of political authority was the construction of a dense system of issue-specific institutions or regimes (see Chapter 2), and economic institutions were central to this system. Believing that the Great Depression of the 1930s had contributed to WWII, the victorious allied powers constructed an ambitious framework of multilateral institutions to manage the world economy, which came to be known as the Bretton Woods system. These included, first, the International Bank for Reconstruction and Development (the World Bank) and the IMF, and in 1948 the GATT, which in 1995 became the WTO. Reflecting a bargain between the US and Britain, and the unsung influence of developing states, such as China, India, and Brazil (well-documented by Eric Helleiner), the system sought to ensure the stability of the international monetary system and to foster free trade. To achieve the first, a system of fixed exchange rates was established, in which states agreed to 'peg' the value of their currencies to the value of the US dollar, which was in turn tied to the value of gold (at US\$35 per ounce). The IMF's job was to support this system, helping stricken states to sustain the value of their currencies by providing emergency loans. Free trade was pursued under the GATT, which committed states to the managed and coordinated reduction of national tariffs. For the best part of three decades, these institutions successfully stabilized the

international monetary system and opened global trade, with
average national tariffs falling to less than 20 per cent.

The original Bretton Woods system collapsed in the early 1970s,
when in 1971 President Richard Nixon unilaterally abolished the
dollar–gold standard, effectively destroying the fixed exchange
rate system. By this time, the European and Japanese economies
had recovered from WWII and emerged as major competitors
to the US. Meanwhile, the US economy was burdened by
the escalating costs of the Vietnam War and, from 1973, by the
OPEC-induced surge in oil prices, mentioned earlier. As the trade
balance shifted away from the US, its competitors accumulated
large reserves of US dollars, and when Washington could no
longer sustain its commitment to convert these to gold, Nixon
abandoned the system. This prompted a major shift in the
management of the international monetary system. The world
moved quickly toward a system of floating exchange rates, giving
national central banks and international currency markets
responsibility for the stability of monetary relations. Many see this
as a shift away from multilateral, rule-based regulation toward
decentralized cooperation and 'club standards'. The inadequacies
of this approach were starkly exposed by the 2008 GFC.
Insufficient regulation had allowed US banks to make enormous
numbers of risky housing loans, and when housing prices started
falling after 2006, US banks and other investors suffered huge
losses, as did foreign banks who had invested heavily in the US
housing market.

Initially, the trading side of the Bretton Woods system fared much
better than the monetary side. The GATT went through successive
rounds of renegotiation, gradually reducing average tariffs in
member states and restricting non-tariff barriers to trade, such as
subsidies and import quotas. This was capped off by the 1995
transformation of the GATT into the WTO, a formal international
organization with an expanded responsibility for trade in services
and intellectual property rights, as well as manufactured and

agricultural goods. The momentum of multilateral trade regulation stalled, however, with the still unconcluded Doha round of negotiations (started in 2001), where, in a range of disputes, developing countries have taken a stand against the continued unfair trading practices of rich, developed states, particularly the subsidizing of agriculture and the widespread use of non-tariff barriers (such as protections on intellectual property rights). A notable consequence of this has been the recent proliferation of separate bilateral and regional free trade agreements.

Developments in trade and monetary governance have thus converged somewhat. In both cases, the balance has shifted from multilateral rule-based regulation to decentralized cooperation. Added to this, the reliance on market mechanisms to ensure monetary stability is matched in the area of trade by the increased rights that bilateral and regional agreements are granting to private actors, such as multinational corporations. For example, one of the most controversial elements of one such agreement, the failed Trans-Pacific Partnership, would have given multinational corporations the right to sue national governments in foreign courts for breaches of contract (a right substantially diluted in the replacement agreement, the Comprehensive and Progressive Agreement for Trans-Pacific Partnership, CPTPP).

Important as international institutions and regulations have been in shaping the global economy, in a worldwide system of states, the sovereign state remains the most influential unit of political authority. Yet states come in different forms, and they use their political authority differently to stimulate and structure their economies (or their parts of the global economy). Moreover, within states, and also in the politics of global economic governance, how political authority ought to relate to the economy is hotly contested. The simple distinction between democracies and authoritarian states helps us little here, as historically the way states in each category have managed their economies has varied greatly. During the Cold War it was common to distinguish between three kinds of state–economy relations: the *market economies* of Western capitalist states, which, to different degrees, sought to harness the competitive dynamics of a free market; the *command economies* of the communist bloc, where the state controlled the factories and farms, determined the nature and prices of what was produced, and dictated personal incomes; and the diverse *planned economies* instituted in Africa, East and South Asia, and Latin America, where the state defined national economic objectives, intervened to direct economic activity, and often owned key financial and manufacturing industries. The world was not quite this simple of course, as great variation and overlap existed within each of these categories. For instance, much has been written about the differences between Western market economies, with a common distinction drawn between the liberal market economies of states like the US, Britain, and Australia, and coordinated market economies, such as Germany, Japan, and Sweden.

Many of these forms of state–economy relations did not survive the 1980s and the end of the Cold War. Compelled by the policies of the IMF and World Bank (which made loans conditional on the deregulation of national economies), and reflecting national ideological and political changes, developing countries abandoning their campaign for an NIEO and, to various degrees, shifted from planned to more liberal market economies. After the economic and political disasters of Mao Zedong's Great Leap Forward and the Cultural Revolution, China embarked on the reform and opening of its economy, combining centralized planning with the privatization of key industries, greater reliance on the free market, the encouragement of foreign direct investment, and participation in multilateral economic institutions. The end of communism in Eastern Europe and the 1991 collapse of the Soviet Union saw the demise of the most prominent command economies and the vigorous promotion of Western-backed models of market-led economic governance.

The net effect of all of these changes was a general liberalizing of the world economy, and the narrowing of differences between forms of state–economy relations, with most states lying somewhere between planned market economies and liberal market economies. The 2008 GFC placed this model under considerable strain, however, sparking intense debate within states and internationally about over-reliance on market self-regulation, especially in the area of finance, and the need for greater state intervention in the economy to moderate cycles of economic boom and bust. Yet many commentators have observed how little has changed. New international regulations on global finance have been modest at best, and with the exception of the Trump Administration's tariff war with China, most states have remained committed to free and open markets, and have favoured tough austerity measures to deal with national debt over increased government spending to stimulate their economies.

Challenges ahead

Earlier in this chapter, I stressed the mutual dependence of economies and political authority. Economies are not self-regulating or sustaining, they depend on political authority, and political authority—legitimate political power—depends on a functioning economy. At the very same time, however, that there has been a global convergence around more market-led modes of economic governance—evident in the shift from multilateral rule-based regulation to decentralized cooperation and private authority, and in the move globally toward national market economies—the ability of these modes to deliver social and economic goods faces profound challenges, of which four stand out.

To begin with, the financialization and digitalization of the global economy are producing new actors, products, markets, patterns of work, and distributions of wealth. And maximizing the benefits of these changes while limiting their social costs and disruptions requires adroit political choices and institutional innovation, not simple reliance on market mechanisms.

Second, increasing economic inequality has emerged as a major test of political legitimacy, both for national governments and for international institutions. Since the 1980s economic inequalities have grown in almost all national economies; and globally, while the poorest 50 per cent of the world's population have struggled to secure more than 10 per cent of global income, the share earned by the richest 1 per cent grew from 16 to 20 per cent (see World Inequality Lab, *World Inequality Report 2018*). When combined with shifts in the nature and location of industry, and with the economic austerity many states instituted after the GFC, such inequality has led many to question the will and/or capacity of existing political parties and institutions to distribute fairly the economic benefits of globalization.

Third, the relationship between economic management and legitimate political power is now inextricably connected to today's global environmental crisis. Addressing the climate and biodiversity emergencies requires far-reaching economic change, to modes of consumption, forms of energy generation, types of industry and agriculture, the nature and place of work, means of transport and scope of travel, and more. Yet efforts to institute such changes have met with fierce political contestation, both within many states and internationally, which raises serious questions about the adaptive capacities of existing political and economic institutions.

Finally, all of the above challenges require global political leadership, especially if new international institutions are to be designed and constructed. Yet with the Trump administration's antipathy toward multilateralism, Europe's preoccupation with the crisis in the EU, and uncertainties about China's will, capacity, and objectives, it is unclear where such leadership will come from, individually or collectively. Interestingly, it is the Group of Twenty

(G20), which includes leading Western and non-Western economies, that has emerged as the principal 'club-style' vehicle for coordinating economic policy globally.

Whether these challenges can be met is far from certain. What each shows, however, is that global economic life and international relations—understood as the global organization of political authority—are, and will remain, fundamentally interwoven.

Chapter 6
Rights

Human rights often appear in textbooks as just one among a number of important issue-areas, like the environment or nuclear proliferation. This reflects the widespread assumption that although they are an important feature of contemporary world politics, they are not central to the dynamics of the international system. Indeed, we think about human rights in a very particular way. We imagine a system of sovereign states, generated by the forces of war and economic competition, and then see human rights as a post-1945 (or even post-1970s) innovation designed to civilize states, to prevent them preying on their own peoples. Commentators disagree about how successful that innovation has been, but this is the dominant way of thinking about human rights.

This chapter presents a different view. Individual rights, of which human rights are one form, have been central to the evolution of today's global organization of political authority. I am not claiming here that human rights, as universal moral principles, have swept the world before them and that the forces of darkness are in retreat. Far from it. Rather, I am arguing that struggles for individual rights have shaped the global organization of political authority in two crucial ways. First, over the course of five centuries, these struggles helped transform a world of empires into today's global system of sovereign states. Second, in the latter phases of this process, struggles for human rights drove the codification of legally binding international human rights norms, effectively qualifying the rights—and thus political authority—of sovereign states. Moreover, in diverse contexts, from Latin America and Eastern Europe to established liberal democracies, human rights campaigns have mobilized these norms to bring states to heel.

The following discussion begins by explaining the centrality of rights to all configurations of political authority, the nature of individual rights (and in turn human rights), and the role individual rights play as 'power-mediators'. I then show how struggles for individual rights reshaped the global organization of political authority, fragmenting successive empires and licensing the construction of sovereign states. The final section examines the post-1945 development of the international human rights regime, and how the norms of this regime have been mobilized in efforts to constrain abuses of state power.

Political authority and individual rights

All arrangements of political authority—be they local or large-scale; sovereign, imperial, or heteronomous—distribute social and political entitlements, or what we now call 'rights'. Indeed, one could argue that configurations of political authority are glued together by such rights, and that the nature of these rights, and how they are distributed, tells us an enormous amount about how political authority is organized.

As we saw in Chapter 2, today's global system of states divides political authority into territorial units, and these units enjoy sovereign rights, like the right to supreme authority within their borders. Yet today the scope of sovereign rights—the powers that a state can legitimately claim—is conditioned by the political rights of the individuals within its borders. Where individuals have robust political rights, sovereign rights are qualified, and vice versa.

If individuals have the rights to freedom of expression and association, for example, the state has no sovereign right to detain them for marching in the streets and criticizing the government. The same is true of non-sovereign arrangements of political authority. The heteronomous political order of medieval Europe also distributed political entitlements, even if not couched in the language of rights. The multiple centres of political authority—the Holy Roman Empire, the Catholic Church, the various monarchies and principalities, cities and municipalities, and local feudal lords—all had distinctive political and social rights. So too, however, did the individuals who fell under their jurisdictions, from the peasants to merchants. In both of these cases—the sovereign and the heteronomous—how the rights of individuals and political actors or institutions have been defined, and how they have stood in relation to one another, has affected the nature and scope of political authority.

Of course, as this discussion already indicates, rights vary greatly. It is common to distinguish between individual and collective rights: the rights of sole persons (like you or me), and the rights of groups (such as indigenous peoples, like the Yanomami people of the Amazon). Because of limited space, I focus here on individual rights alone.

Individual rights come in two forms: general and special rights. Special rights arise from contracts, customs, or the social positions we hold. When you buy a house, for example, the contract of sale gives you certain special rights (like the right to purchase the property for a set amount, and to take ownership on a set date), rights you don't have outside of that contract. The political entitlements of medieval individuals—Popes, monarchs, and burghers—were also special: they came from their positions in the complex heteronomous political and social order. General rights are very different, and they are the ones that most concern us here. Individuals have general rights not because of contracts they sign or positions they occupy, but because of their status as particular kinds of beings. There are different versions of this argument, but all hold that there is something unique and valuable about human individuals, and that they have certain rights to protect these qualities, rights that they have automatically and that cannot be taken away (even if they can be violated). One argument says that individuals are unique in their abilities to imagine good lives, and that general rights protect their capacity to pursue these visions. Another argument holds that individuals have basic needs (from food and shelter to free expression), and if these needs are not met, individuals cannot live fully human lives. This is why individuals have general, inalienable rights: to help ensure these needs are met.

You will notice that so far I have refrained from using the language of 'human rights', despite talking about rights that individuals have simply because they are particular kinds of beings, with particular capacities and needs that warrant protection. Aren't these human rights? Yes and no. Human rights are certainly general individual rights. They are rights we have solely because of our status as special, valuable types of beings— human beings. Yet the idea that general individual rights apply to all biological humans is very recent: an achievement of the post-1945 era. Before that, it was standard practice for individuals to assert their inherent and inalienable rights while denying that other humans—women, workers who lacked property, slaves, colonized and indigenous people, and more—were 'rational adults' entitled to such rights. Two crucial things flow from this. First, unless we wish to obscure these exclusions, we should use the term 'human rights' only for the most recent phase in the evolution of general individual rights, when it was accepted, often reluctantly, that they are rights held by *all* biological humans. Second, we need to recognize that the history of individual rights has been marked by recurrent struggles over who, among all biological humans, is entitled to such rights (from the anti-slavery movement to today's campaigns for lesbian, gay, bisexual, transgender, queer, and intersex (LGBTQI) rights), and that these struggles have been closely associated with major shifts in the global organization of political authority.

Why are individual rights—or human rights—valuable? Why do individuals want their rights recognized and respected? One reason is that over time individual rights have become what the eminent legal philosopher Ronald Dworkin called normative 'trump cards', they win against all other moral considerations. They have become the dominant language of right and wrong, and to claim that basic human rights are being violated is one of the strongest accusations that can be made against an actor or institution. As the moral philosopher Joel Feinberg put it, 'rights are especially strong objects to "stand upon", a most useful sort of moral furniture'.

Another reason is that individual rights are power-mediators: they are moral principles that individuals who are materially weak can invoke in an effort to change the power relationship between themselves and materially powerful actors or institutions that seek to do them harm (the tortured seeking to stay the hand of the torturer, for example). This is what John Locke, the great 17th-century liberal political philosopher, meant when he described the natural right to freedom as a 'fence against tyranny'. Once we understand this about individual rights—that their purpose is to mediate power—we can see why they breed antagonistic politics. Because individual rights are always invoked to alter existing power relations, they threaten prevailing institutions of political authority, practices of rule, and related social hierarchies. Not surprisingly, struggles for individual rights frequently meet with severe, often violent, repression.

Rights, empire, and sovereignty

Today's global system of sovereign states is a product of empire and imperial collapse. Until the second half of the 20th century, an evolving system of sovereign states was embedded in a broader system of empires. As we have seen, these two systems were deeply interconnected, as many leading states were also imperial powers (think of Spain, the Netherlands, Portugal, France, and Britain). From this perspective, empire had an integrative effect, entwining European and non-European peoples in complex webs of political, economic, and cultural relations. It was the collapse of the world of empires, however, that ultimately produced our present global system of states. Elsewhere I argue that the system of states spread across the globe in five great waves of expansion, each involving the fragmentation of one or more empires. The first is associated with the end of the European wars of religion and the Peace of Westphalia (1648), the second with the collapse of the Spanish and Portuguese empires and the independence of Latin America countries (1808–25), the third with the end of WWI and the Versailles settlement (1919), the fourth with post-1945 decolonization (1945–70), and the fifth with the break-up of the Soviet Union and Yugoslavia (1992). Of these, the first, second, and fourth are most important, as together they produced most of today's sovereign states and gave the global system its principal regions: the Americas, Africa, Asia, Europe, and the Pacific.

While each of these waves had its own distinctive features, they have things in common as well. All empires are hierarchies: they distribute political authority unequally between an empire's metropolitan core and its colonial periphery (between the UK and British India, for example). These hierarchies distribute political rights and entitlements unequally. If you were a Bengali subject of the British Empire in 1900, you had different rights from a property-owning man in Manchester, who had different rights again from a propertied woman in Cambridge. The legitimacy of empires depended on the stability of these unequal entitlements. Yet in the three most important waves of expansion mentioned above—those associated with Westphalia, Latin American independence, and post-1945 decolonization—these entitlements were challenged by struggles for general individual rights. At first these struggles merely sought imperial reform, the recognition of subject peoples' rights through institutional change. But in each case, when empires refused such reforms, often heightening repression, the struggles radicalized, ultimately seeking sovereign independence.

The 1648 Peace of Westphalia consists of two main treaties, the Treaty of Osnabrück and the Treaty of Münster. Together these brought an end to over a century of religious conflict in Europe, conflict driven by the Protestant Reformation and the Catholic Counter-Reformation. Most accounts of Westphalia pay insufficient attention to this context, but it is essential to understanding the nature of the Peace. The Reformation challenged the religious authority of the Catholic Church, and this in turn undercut the political authority of the Holy Roman Empire, the self-proclaimed guardian of Latin Christendom. Critical here was the Protestant belief that individuals gain salvation through faith alone, which was directly at odds with the Catholic view that salvation came from faith and good works (something the Catholic Church facilitated). Not only did this make the ability to freely exercise one's faith essential to salvation, it threatened to cut the Catholic Church out of the salvation business. The centrality of this issue to the devastating 'Wars of Religion' is evident in the various attempts to negotiate peace. The 1541 and 1546 Diets (Assemblies) of Regensburg, which Emperor Charles V convened to reunite Latin Christendom, fell apart over this issue of salvation. The 1555 Peace of Augsburg is renowned for giving princes the right to define the religions of their territories, but quickly collapsed because it failed to protect individuals' liberty of religious conscience. Only in 1648, after the most recent phase of warfare had killed an estimated eight million people, did the Peace of Westphalia settle the conflict.

The old idea that Westphalia created the modern system of states has been widely critiqued. However, the treaties did three crucial things: they greatly diminished the political authority of the Holy Roman Emperor; they invested the 'Electors, Princes, and States' of the empire with many of the rights we now associate with sovereignty; and they upheld the rights of individuals to liberty of religious conscience, thus qualifying the rights of emerging sovereigns. In these ways, the impact of the treaties is still felt today.

Between 1808 and 1825 the Spanish and Portuguese empires in Latin America collapsed, producing seventeen new sovereign states. I focus here on the crisis in the Spanish Empire, as it produced fifteen of these new states. The crisis was sparked by Napoleon's invasion of Spain in 1807–8, and the subsequent installation of his brother Joseph as King of Spain and the Indies. In response, anti-Napoleonic insurgencies broke out across the empire. While their primary objectives were the defeat of France and returning Ferdinand VII to the throne, the many liberals in their ranks also sought to reform the empire. They did not want a return to absolute rule; they wanted a constitutional monarchy, in which individuals were represented politically. In 1810 the insurgents established a General Cortes (or parliament) in Cadiz, a principal purpose of which was the negotiation of a post-Napoleonic constitution for Spain.

A fundamental division soon emerged between delegates from peninsular Spain and those from the Americas. Most agreed that it was individuals who needed political representation, but they disagreed over who, among all humans living in the empire, counted as rights-worthy individuals: 'rational adults', in the language of the day. Peninsular Spaniards held that only those of Spanish blood qualified, whereas the Americans fought to include Indians and freed slaves (originally brought from Africa as part of the slave trade). On every key vote the Americans were defeated, and the resulting 1812 Constitution of Cadiz, widely hailed then as the most liberal in Europe, denied many Americans the most basic rights of political representation. To this point, most of the American insurgents were reformers not revolutionaries, but Cadiz had a radicalizing effect, fuelling wars for sovereign independence across the Americas. By 1825 the empire was finished, and what had been a largely European system of states, dominated by monarchies, was transformed by the addition of a host of new Latin American republics.

Between 1946 and 1975 all of Europe's remaining empires collapsed, producing seventy-six new sovereign states. More than this, the institution of empire itself collapsed. In 1945, when the UN Charter was negotiated, empire was still described as a 'sacred trust', but by 1960 the UN Declaration on the Granting of Independence to Colonial Countries and Peoples declared empire a 'crime'. Many reasons have been suggested for this dramatic transformation, from the post-1945 weakness of the imperial powers to the strength of local anti-colonial struggles. A viable explanation has to be able to explain, first, the rapid and simultaneous collapse of multiple empires, and second, the loss of legitimacy of empire itself as a form of political authority. The second is the key to the first. And to understand how empire was delegitimized, we have to turn to the politics of human rights.

For empire to be discredited, colonialized peoples in Asia, Africa, and the Pacific first had to establish their right to self-determination. But until WWII this right applied only to ethnically-defined nations, and only to those in Europe. If the right to self-determination was to be of any use to colonized peoples, it had to be reconstituted and mobilized anew. This was achieved by the newly independent, post-colonial members of the fledgling UN, who used its new human rights forums to redefine self-determination as a prerequisite for the enjoyment of all other human rights.

There is a widespread myth that post-1945 codification of international human rights was a Western project, but in reality post-colonial states, like Egypt, India, and Mexico, played a crucial role. In the long negotiation of the legally binding Covenants on 'Civil and Political Rights' and 'Economic, Social and Cultural

Rights' these states consistently argued for the priority of civil and political rights, led the push for strong enforcement mechanisms, and successfully defeated Western efforts to prevent the treaties applying to Europe's colonies. Having secured the universality of international human rights norms, post-colonial states then cast the right to self-determination as essential to the protection of all other human rights. Not only did they succeed in having this right enshrined in the two Covenants, Article 1 of the 1960 UN Declaration on the Granting of Independence to Colonial Countries and Peoples stated that 'subjection of peoples to alien subjugation, domination and exploitation constitutes a denial of fundamental human rights'. By that point, the institution of empire was morally bankrupt, and after 1960, as I have shown elsewhere, the rate of decolonization tripled, jumping from 1.3 states per year to 3.9. This rapidly produced today's global system of sovereign states, fundamentally transforming international relations.

Human rights and state conduct

The struggles for individual rights discussed above imagined the sovereign state as a protector of such rights, as a desirable institutional alternative to the tyranny of empire. The spread of sovereign states across the globe has exposed the naiveté of such ideas. Human rights need institutions to recognize and protect them. Individuals may have such rights simply by virtue of being human, but without protective institutions they will always be vulnerable to violation. It is abundantly clear, however, that while the sovereign state *can* provide such protection, often this is wanting. Indeed, one could argue quite reasonably that sovereign states are the principal violators of human rights, and by a long margin. From the Nazi Holocaust to Myanmar's current genocidal persecution of its Muslim Rohingya people, history is replete with examples. Not surprisingly, at the very same time that sovereign states were replacing the last of Europe's empires, efforts were under way to construct international protections for human rights, from codified international norms to judicial mechanisms.

The centrepiece of these institutions is the International Bill of Rights. This comprises the Universal Declaration of Human Rights; the ICCPR; the International Covenant on Economic, Social and Cultural Rights (ICESCR); and the optional protocols to these Covenants. Proclaimed in 1948, the Universal Declaration sets out 'the equal and inalienable rights' of all humans 'as a common standard of achievement for all peoples and all nations'. Setting out core civil and political rights, on the one hand, and key economic and social rights, on the other, the Declaration was not intended to be legally binding. It is the two International Covenants, adopted in 1966 and coming into force in 1976, that form the legally binding core of the Bill of Rights. Originally only one covenant was planned, but states disagreed about whether civil and political rights and economic and social rights were of the same kind, and about which was primary. They eventually agreed to negotiate separate covenants, one on civil and political rights, the other on economic and social rights. This is often cast as a Western/non-Western divide, but as noted above, leading post-colonial states agreed that civil and political rights took precedence. Moreover, India's support for two covenants reflected the separation of these rights in its own constitution, where civil and political rights and economic and social rights were differentiated, as only the former was considered prosecutable in a court of law.

While these treaties form the legal core of the international human rights regime, they are nested within a number of other important covenants and conventions. The post-1945 move to codify international human rights was driven, in significant measure, by the atrocities of the Nazi Holocaust. Not surprisingly, one of the earliest legally binding human rights treaties was the 1948 Convention on the Prevention and Punishment of the Crime of Genocide (CPPCG), which defines genocide as a crime under international law, specifies genocidal acts, and sets out the responsibilities of its signatories. The 1970s and 1980s saw the adoption of a second wave of human rights instruments, of which three are especially important. The 1979 CEDAW requires signatories to legally prohibit discrimination against women, ensure that women's rights have the same legal protections as men's, take all necessary measures to eliminate discrimination, and submit regular progress reports to the Committee on the Elimination of Discrimination against Women. Both the Universal Declaration and the ICCPR had established the individual's right not to be tortured, but the 1984 Convention against Torture and Other Cruel, Inhumane or Degrading Treatment (CAT) requires signatories to prevent torture within their territories, specifies that no extraordinary circumstances, including war, justify torture, and obliges signatories to lodge regular progress reports with the Committee against Torture. Lastly, the 1989 Convention on the Rights of the Child (CRC) clarifies that the International Bill of Rights applies to children as well as adults, and goes further to specify rights that are peculiar to children, reflecting their particular vulnerabilities and developmental needs.

A major criticism of these instruments is that although they are legally binding on their signatories they have weak, even non-existent, enforcement mechanisms. As we have seen, most have oversight committees as part of the UN, in some cases individuals can petition these committees directly, and the committees regularly issue robust criticisms of states' human rights records. But beyond this, the treaty system itself has little formal capacity to enforce compliance. Such capacity does exist, but in key regional human rights systems and in the recent development of international courts and tribunals. The European human rights system is the strongest. Founded on the 1950 European Convention on Human Rights (ECHR), the system includes the powerful European Court of Human Rights, which hears applications from both states and individuals, and whose decisions are legally binding. Global human rights courts did not exist until the Rome Statute of the ICC took effect in 2002. Based in The Hague, the ICC investigates and tries individuals charged with genocide, war crimes, crimes against humanity, and the crime of aggression, most of which involve gross violations of human rights. In the 1990s the UN created two temporary tribunals—the International Criminal Tribunal for the Former Yugoslavia (1993–2017), and the International Criminal Tribunal for Rwanda (1995–2015)—but there was a widespread perception that the world needed a permanent court for the trial of mass atrocity crimes, and the ICC was created in response. As we saw in Chapter 3, though, the Court has proven highly controversial.

The old way of conceiving international relations—where states are the principal actors, and attention focuses on their external relations with one another—struggles to accommodate international human rights. Why would states ever codify rights that are designed to qualify their sovereign authority and limit what they can do to the individuals within their borders? And how, if states are the actors that matter, do international human rights norms ever make any difference (which thankfully at times they do)? The answers to such questions are surprisingly straightforward: the role of non-state actors has been crucial. States certainly signed and ratified the above treaties, and often enlightened states have helped push human rights agendas and make treaties more than they might otherwise have been. But in general, states have been led, corralled, and shamed into action by non-state actors, often networks of local activists, transnational human rights movements, and international organizations. It is these actors and organizations, not the efforts of states, that have given life to the international human rights regime, making it a dynamic site of political struggle and change.

How, then, have non-state actors successfully advanced human rights? Considerable research has been done on how 'transnational advocacy networks' of local activists, transnational

Rights

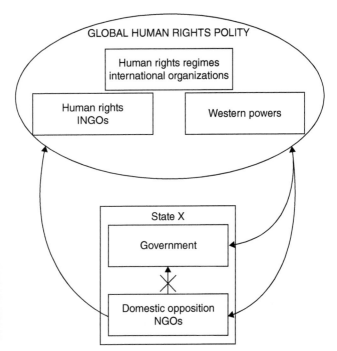

6. The 'Boomerang Pattern' of transnational influence.

human rights groups, and international organizations (like the UN), have changed the policies and practices of sovereign states. Two arguments have been particularly influential. The first, advanced by the American political scientists Margaret Keck and Kathryn Sikkink, holds that the relationship between pressure from transnational networks and change in states' human rights practices follows a 'Boomerang' pattern. As Figure 6 shows, when working alone, domestic human rights groups get blocked when trying to achieve change in states violating human rights. But when they reach outside their states, publicizing violations to other states and international organizations, they can build transnational advocacy networks, mobilize international human rights norms, and bring external pressure to bear on their rights-abusing states. Like a boomerang, local activists throw their human rights concerns into the global arena and it returns in the form of international scrutiny and condemnation, often compelling violator states to reform their practices. The efficacy of these processes has been demonstrated in many cases, one of which is the demise of apartheid in South Africa. As Audie Klotz, one of the leading scholars in this area, explains, anti-apartheid activists, in association with newly independent 'front-line' African states, worked within international organizations, especially the UN and the Commonwealth of Nations, to mobilize the emerging norm against racism, compel Britain, France, and the US (South Africa's biggest supporters) to institute sanctions, and eventually compel the 1991 abolition of apartheid.

Illuminating as it might be, the 'Boomerang' argument seems to suggest that one cycle—one throw of the boomerang—is sufficient to bring meaningful change in a state's human rights practices. In reality, human rights changes come in phases, produced over time through repeated cycles of pressure and reform. To capture this, in 1999 Thomas Risse, Stephen Ropp, and Kathryn Sikkink proposed a 'spiral model' of human rights change. As Figure 7 details, the spiral circles through five phases, each producing a deeper level of change. From the initial condition of repression, states can be pushed, first, to deny that they are committing any abuses, then to make 'tacit concessions' to human rights activists, eventually to accept international human rights norms (by ratifying treaties and making domestic legal changes), and, finally, to protect human rights consistently. Risse, Ropp, and Sikkink, along with their fellow contributors, showed this process at work across a wide range of cases, spanning Africa, Eastern Europe, Latin America, and South-East Asia.

More recent research has shown the limits of this perspective on global human rights change. Admitting that they paid insufficient attention to the way states comply with human rights norms,

The columns are headed:

Society | **State** | **International/Transnational**

Society:
- Weak domestic opposition
- Domestic opposition
- Mobilization and strengthening of groups engaging human rights norms
- New domestic actors and sustained links to transnational networks
- Normative appeals
- Information
- Expansion in new political space
- Human rights assuming centre stage in societal discourse

State:
1. **Repression**
2. **Denial** — Repressive state denies validity of human rights norms as subject to international juristiction, claims non-intervention norm
3. **Tactical concessions**
   - Concessions to the human rights network
   - Reduced margin of manoeuvre re human rights

   Policy change   Regime change
4. **Prescriptive status** — State accepts international norm
   - Ratifies international treaties
   - Institutionalizes norms domestically
   - Discursive practices
5. **Rule-consistent behaviour**

International/Transnational:
Transnational networks
- Receive information from domestic opposition
- Invoke international human rights norms
- Pressurize repressive state
- Mobilize international organizations and liberal states

Sustained bilateral and multilateral network pressure

Reduced network mobilization

(left margin, rotated) International Relations

7. The 'Spiral Model' of human rights change.

98

Risse, Ropp, and Sikkink have gone on to revise their argument. They now hold that getting states to comply often requires a mixture of coercion (such as economic sanctions), positive incentives (like international recognition for improvements in human rights practices), persuasion (through international human rights forums), and capacity building (such as the reform of national legal institutions). Others have gone further, arguing that we need to look beyond state compliance with human rights norms to how those norms are actually implemented. Many of the human rights conventions discussed above oblige signatory states to adopt national human rights legislation. States will have complied if they pass such legislation, but as Alexander Betts and Phil Orchard have recently argued, this does not mean that human rights norms have been implemented, that they 'actually make a difference to people's lives "on the ground"…'. Whether states implement their human rights commitments depends on a number of factors: from cultural and legal conditions (such as local norms about gender equality or the availability of legal aid), through state capacity and the interests of key actors (like ruling political parties and the security forces), to the nature and working of national bureaucracies (including their willingness and ability to process claims of human rights violations).

Another strand of new research is showing that human rights change is not always a unilinear, progressive process. Advances can be reversed. For example, the strengthening of international norms on gender equality, and moves in many states to bolster and protect women's rights, has provoked a conservative backlash and serious legislative reversals. Russia's recent decriminalization of certain forms of domestic violence is a case in point. The story is similar with LGBTQI rights, where in many states, especially in Eastern Europe, recent protections have been rolled back. Finally, the recent resurgence of authoritarianism globally has highlighted the capacities that recalcitrant states (or their leaders), especially great powers, have to resist boomerang processes of human rights change. Some of these are old—like killing or detaining local human rights activists—but others are new, like the use of cyber surveillance to stifle dissent, block the transnational flow of knowledge, and propagate disinformation.

These debates neglect one of the most significant aspects of the international politics of human rights over the past two decades: debates concerning the use of force to prevent extreme violations of human rights, in particular ethnic cleansing and genocide. The post-Cold War era has seen stunning failures of international resolve and action, most notably the 1994 Rwandan genocide, and highly controversial instances of humanitarian intervention, particularly in Kosovo (1999) and Libya (2011). But as noted in Chapter 4, this period has also seen the development of the doctrine of R2P. Another achievement of transnational advocacy networks, this doctrine, which was formally endorsed by the UN in 2005, specifies that the sovereign authority of states is dependent on their responsibility to protect their peoples, and that the international community has responsibility to provide such protection when states fail in their responsibility. While controversy surrounds the meaning and application of this new understanding of sovereignty, it is a significant site in which the relationship between human rights and national and international political authority is being negotiated.

Some scholars, like the legal historian Samuel Moyn, argue that the era of international human rights was very short-lived, that it took off only in the 1970s and is now rapidly fading. Such views depend, first, on a denial that human rights played any role in post-1945 decolonization, and second, that the power and leadership of the US was essential to their post-1970s development. As we have seen, however, both of these positions are flawed. The politics of individual rights was deeply implicated in the gradual development of today's global systems of sovereign states—not least in 20th-century decolonization—and the codification and mobilization of international human rights norms has been driven principally by actors other than the

US: newly independent post-colonial states, enlightened middle powers, and transnational advocacy networks. In all of this, the politics of individual/human rights has had a major impact on international relations, shaping and reshaping the global organization of political authority.

Chapter 7
Culture

The politics of culture looms large in contemporary international relations, as diverse actors—from states to transnational insurgents—are mobilizing around ethnic, racial, religious, and civilizational identities, values, and grievances. Rising states, such as China and India, are not just challenging Western economic and military power; they are also contesting Western cultural dominance, fashioning themselves as distinctive kinds of civilizational powers, animated by their own unique cultural histories, values, and practices. Meanwhile, ethnic nationalism is on the rise across the world, with its signature attacks on globally-oriented elites, cultural minorities, and immigrants and refugees. And if this weren't enough, new forms of transnational terrorism threaten many societies, justifying violence in the name of politicized religion or racial supremacy. Together, these developments challenge the long-held view that international relations had been successfully secularized, and that culture had been rendered a domestic affair.

What implications does all of this have for the global organization of the political authority? For some realists, who think that international relations is simply a struggle for material power, this cultural turmoil is a distraction, turning our attention away from the real drivers of politics: power and interests. Two other views dominate contemporary debate, however. The first is 'culturalist', and holds that culture has a profound effect on how political authority is organized. Arrangements of political authority reflect deep cultural values, and shared values sustain political institutions. From this perspective, today's cultural diversity is a problem, as it erodes the Western cultural foundations of the modern international order. The main alternative to this view is 'institutionalist'. It denies that cultural diversity is a problem, arguing that the modern international order has developed institutions—from sovereignty to multilateralism—that neutralize the political effects of cultural difference, enabling culturally different states and peoples to coexist and interact successfully. Neither of these views adequately captures the complex relationship between culture and the global organization of political authority, however. Culturalists fail to see that large-scale arrangements of political authority have historically always evolved in diverse cultural contexts, and institutionalists misunderstand the role of international institutions: they don't neutralize culture and render it irrelevant, they organize it, as we shall see below.

This chapter offers a different way of thinking about the relationship between culture and the global organization of political authority. It begins by noting the highly contested nature of culture as a concept, before offering (nonetheless) a broad working definition. It then explores in greater detail the deficiencies of the culturalist and institutionalist positions, and maps out an alternative understanding. This view treats cultural diversity as the norm, and holds that all large-scale arrangements of political authority have developed institutions for ordering that diversity, creating distinctive political and cultural hierarchies.

What is culture?

Raymond Williams, perhaps the most influential cultural theorist, notes that culture 'is one of the two or three most complicated words in the English language'. Not only have anthropologists, cultural studies scholars, and sociologists long argued over how to define and study it, in everyday life we use the term in multiple ways. As Terry Eagleton, another leading cultural theorist, explains, we use it to refer to high artistic or intellectual achievements, like the ballet, the opera, and great paintings. Somewhat differently, we use it when referring to processes of spiritual or intellectual development: becoming cultured, so to speak. We also use it, in a third sense, when referring to 'the values, customs, beliefs and symbolic practices by which men and women live'. And, finally, we use it more broadly when referring to a people's whole way of life, including everything from their 'poetry, music and dance' to their 'transport network, system of voting and methods of garbage disposal'.

It is beyond the scope of this short chapter to resolve the ongoing debates about the nature of culture, or to bring order to the many daily ways we use the term. Two moves are helpful, though. First, when thinking about the relationship between culture and the organization of political authority, it is the third and fourth uses of the term that are most relevant: a society's values, beliefs, and practices, or its whole way of life. The equation of culture with a whole way of life is problematic, though. If culture is everything, then it must include the organization of political authority, making it hard to think about the relationship between the two. I thus favour a version of the former conception of culture, defining it broadly as shared ideas, beliefs, norms, and values. These are expressed though, and embedded within, language, images, bodies, artefacts, and practices. And they shape social life by informing the identities and interests of individuals and groups, and by providing resources that help actors pursue their diverse ends and purposes. Our understandings of ourselves are profoundly affected by the complex cultural environments we inhabit, but we also rely—often unconsciously, but sometimes consciously—on values, norms, and practices from these environments to help us do things (from arranging a wedding to running a political campaign) and to justify what we want to achieve.

The second move is to see culture as always complex and often contradictory. As we will see below, culturalists also see culture as shared ideas, values, and practices, but imagine these as forming coherent, tightly integrated, and neatly bounded 'cultures': commonly thought of as nations, religions, civilizations. For at least thirty years, however, anthropologists, cultural studies scholars, and sociologists have treated culture as far more complex. As eminent sociologist Ann Swidler puts it, 'all real cultures contain diverse, often conflicting symbols, rituals, stories, and guides to action'. And, as Nobel Prize winning economist Amartya Sen argues, this complex cultural universe gives individuals multiple identities.

> The same person can be, without any contradiction, an American citizen, of Caribbean origin, with African ancestry, a Christian, a liberal, a woman, a vegetarian, a long-distance runner, a historian, a schoolteacher, a novelist, a feminist, a heterosexual, a believer in gay and lesbian rights, a theater lover, an environmental activist, a tennis fan, a jazz musician, and someone who is deeply committed to the view that there are intelligent beings in outer space with whom it is extremely urgent to talk (preferably in English).

Culturalists and institutionalists

How does culture affect the nature, stability, and operation of large-scale configurations of political authority, like systems of sovereign states or empires? The contrasting ways that culturalists and institutionalists answer this question highlights their essential differences. Culturalists hold that all systems of political authority require strong cultural foundations. One of the clearest statements of this position was provided by Martin Wight, a leading figure in the English School we discussed in Chapter 2. Wight claimed that 'a states-system will not come into being without a degree of cultural unity among its members', and when discussing the Ancient Greek, Chinese, and Western systems, he held that 'each arose in a single culture'. For culturalists like

Wight, strong, coherent cultural foundations are thought to do two things: they inform how political authority is organized—the nature of political institutions and practices—and they secure the legitimacy of these arrangements, because they embody cultural values that actors share. It is often claimed, for example, that today's international order is a product of Western civilization; that its institutions are Western cultural artefacts, dependent on the cultural consensus that unites Western powers. Because culturalists place so much emphasis on unified cultural foundations, they see heightened cultural diversity as destabilizing. Wight worried, for example, about the impact that post-1945 decolonization, and the resulting proliferation of non-Western sovereign states, would have on the formerly Western states system, claiming that the expanding system had 'outrun cultural and moral community'. Henry Kissinger, the former US Secretary of State, has expressed a similar view, concerned now about the current rise of non-Western great powers. How, he asks, in today's global system, can 'regions with such diverse cultures, histories, and traditional theories of order vindicate the legitimacy of any common system?'.

Institutionalists are far less worried about the impact of cultural diversity, as they have a very different view of what holds large-scale systems of political authority together. Institutions do this crucial work, they argue, and some of the most important constitutional institutions (see Chapter 2), such as sovereignty, are said to have emerged specifically to deal with problems of cultural diversity. Prior to the 1648 Peace of Westphalia, Europe was devastated by over a century of religious conflict, sparked by the Protestant Reformation. Institutionalists argue that the Westphalian treaties resolved this cultural conflict by instituting a nascent system of sovereign states, in which religion became a domestic affair, as monarchs were authorized to choose the religion practised within their territories (providing it was

Catholicism, Calvinism, or Lutheranism). Institutionalists, like the English School theorist Robert Jackson, hail this as a key moment in the secularization of international relations, a 'pluralist moment' that 'expresses the morality of difference'. Ever since then, it is argued, the institution of sovereignty has provided a robust framework in which states and peoples of different cultures can coexist and cooperate. Indeed, it is upheld by Jackson as 'the most articulate institutional arrangement that humans have yet come up with' for peoples of different cultures to live peaceably side by side. Liberal theorists take this argument one step further, stressing the additional importance of post-1945 fundamental institutions, like international law and multilateralism. John Ikenberry, the leading exponent of this view, argues that these 'liberal' institutions are 'open and rules-based', admitting states of all cultural complexions on the sole condition that they observe the contractual rules of the system. In contrast to culturalists, therefore, who see a unified culture as essential to the survival of international institutions, institutionalists see the health of Westphalian and liberal institutions as essential to the management of cultural difference.

These contrasting views on the relationship between culture and the global organization of political authority are not confined to academic debate, they permeate policy and practice. This is evident in markedly different statements by US Presidents Barack Obama and Donald Trump. Obama is an institutionalist, and in 2014 he called on the UN Security Council to reinvest in international institutions at a time of increased cultural divisions.

> We can renew the international system that has enabled so much progress, or we can allow ourselves to be pulled back into the undertow of instability... And it is no exaggeration to say that humanity's future depends on us uniting against those who would divide us along the fault lines of tribe, sect, race, or religion.

In stark contrast, Trump, a committed culturalist, told a Polish audience that

> [t]he fundamental question of our time is whether the West has the will to survive. Do we have the confidence in our values to defend them at all cost? Do we have enough respect for our citizens to protect our borders? Do we have the desire and the courage to preserve our civilization in the face of those who would subvert or destroy it?

Where Obama saw renewed international institutions as a solution to the problem of cultural division, Trump saw the defence of Western civilization as fundamental.

Although the culturalist and institutionalist positions dominate current debates, both are problematic. The culturalist rests on a flawed understanding of culture and a misreading of history. As we saw above, culture is never unified (as Wight imagined): it is always heterogeneous, contradictory, and never neatly bounded. And if this is true, then culture cannot provide the robust foundations for the organization of political authority that culturalists claim. Not surprisingly, historians of diverse international orders—from the early modern European to the Qing Chinese—have revealed the heterogeneous cultural contexts out of which these orders emerged. The institutionalist view is problematic because it misunderstands the role of institutions. As we will see, international institutions and culture are related in important ways. But institutions do not neutralize culture, rendering it a purely domestic issue, instead they organize culture. They privilege some forms of cultural difference over others (e.g. Catholicism, Calvinism, and Lutheranism were deemed acceptable in the Westphalian settlement but Judaism and Islam were not), and in doing so they create political and cultural hierarchies and patterns of inclusion and exclusion.

Organizing diversity

How, if these perspectives are flawed, should we think about the relationship between culture and the global organization of political authority? A good starting point, I argue elsewhere, is to take seriously what specialists have long told us, that culture is always highly complex and often contradictory. In our everyday lives we are surrounded by, and engage with, a myriad values, beliefs, and practices, ranging from how women and men ought to relate and the proper relationship between religion and politics to the correct behaviour of superiors in the workplace and the treatment of foreigners. In this complex universe, we each develop multiple identities that come to the fore in different ways, in different contexts (I'm a father at parent/teacher meetings, a secular 'greenie' at election time, a professor in front of a class, and a hiker when in the mountains). We navigate the cultural world along with many other people, but often interpret the ideas, values, and practices that swirl around us in very different ways, adding yet another layer of cultural complexity. And if all of this is true of our local cultural worlds—in our villages, towns, cities, and countries—then things only become more complicated at the international level, where the cultural landscape looks anything but homogeneous.

Once we grasp this, we need to ask what implications this always-existing cultural heterogeneity has for the global organization of political authority. I argue elsewhere that heterogeneity poses distinct challenges for those seeking to construct forms of political authority such as sovereign states or empires. In highly complex cultural environments, ideas, values, beliefs, and practices can be harnessed to all manner of political projects. They can be woven into nationalist narratives, enlisted to stoke ethnic separatism, invoked by politicized religious movements, wielded by political parties, used to justify progressive change, harnessed to support human justice, and much, much more. If political elites are to secure and legitimize their power, they have a strong incentive to control what can be done with culture: to define legitimate forms of cultural identification and expression, and to channel and harness these in ways that sustain their own political authority. In other words, in heterogeneous cultural contexts, they are impelled to organize and rule the cultural landscape. To do this, political elites establish what I call 'diversity regimes': norms and practices that simultaneously define the legitimate centres of political power (like sovereign states or empires) and relate these to authorized forms of cultural identity and expression (such as religion, ethnicity, or civilization). Sometimes these regimes are created in great moments of institutional design and construction, at other times they evolve more incrementally.

The best way to understand this is to think about the organization of culture within today's sovereign states. All states seek to shape the cultural terrain within their borders, and they do this by instituting national diversity regimes. Some states have policies of assimilation, where a select national culture is defined and everyone is expected to embrace and internalize this culture (France has long had such a policy). Other states—like Australia and Canada—have multicultural policies, where cultural difference is managed by allowing peoples of diverse cultural backgrounds to retain and express their identities, values, and practices (though usually in ways consistent with the rules and norms of a liberal society). States have instituted far more draconian and brutal diversity regimes as well. Genocide and ethnic-cleansing—from the Nazi Holocaust to recent events in Myanmar—are practices designed to reshape the cultural landscape, albeit through the extermination or expulsion of ethnically, racially, or religiously 'undesirable' communities.

Pointing to national diversity regimes such as these is hardly novel, but the existence of diversity regimes at the international level, in large-scale arrangements of political authority, gets far less attention. Yet they are a crucial feature of such arrangements. In addition to revealing the complex cultural contexts in which the world's most famous sovereign, imperial, and heteronomous orders emerged—such as the Early Modern European system of states and the Roman, Ottoman, and Qing empires—historians have shown the seemingly universal impulse to tame this complexity, to institute diversity regimes that authorize certain forms and expressions of cultural difference and align these with structures of legitimate power.

Two examples illustrate this. The first is the Ottoman Empire (1285–1923), which encompassed peoples of extraordinary cultural diversity. As the distinguished sociologist Karen Barkey explains, the empire 'was not Ottoman, Turkish, or Islamic. It was all of these combined with Roman, Byzantine, Balkan, and Turco-Mongol institutions and practices.' From the outset, Ottoman rulers sought not to extinguish this diversity, but to draw on varied cultural resources to narrate their political legitimacy, and to establish institutions that recognized different religious communities and granted them circumscribed, but legally defined, realms of autonomy. The Ottomans are often noted for their 'millet system', which legally acknowledged Greek Orthodox, Armenian, and Jewish religious communities, recognized their religious institutions as the centres of community life, and used these as administrative channels and vehicles for taxation. As with all long-lived, large-scale arrangements of political authority, the Ottoman Empire saw the rise and fall of several diversity regimes. As prominent international relations scholar Ayse Zarakol explains, long periods of relative toleration were punctuated by phases of significant repression, notably in the 16th and 19th centuries. Interestingly, only in the second of these periods were the persecuted communities non-Muslim. In the 16th century, centralizing Sultans targeted dissenting Muslim communities, suppressing non-Sunni communities and compelling the dominant Sunnis to adopt orthodox, approved religious practices.

The second example is the Qing Chinese Empire (1644–1912). The need to manage cultural diversity was very personal for the Qing, as they themselves were an 'alien' dynasty, 'barbarians' from the Manchurian steppe. The Qing also conquered huge swathes of new territory, expanding China to roughly its present size, drawing under their rule peoples of great cultural diversity. They expanded the boundaries of the former Ming Empire to encompass Manchuria, Mongolia, Tibet, and Xinjiang, all of which were culturally mixed and fluid. As the leading historian Pamela Kyle Crossley observes, these were regions 'in which economic livelihoods, religions, languages, and in many cases gene pools were distributed according to the common routes of commerce, war, pilgrimage and mixed as the flow of goods and peoples determined'. To manage this diversity, the Qing established institutions that simultaneously engaged and reconstituted the varied cultural landscape. They created the Eight Banners system, which tied Manchu, Han, and Mongol ethnicities to the organization of military units, and established the Lifanyuan system, which governed ethnic groups in Inner Asia, thus institutionalizing cultural difference within the imperial administration. The Qing also skilfully cultivated their own cultural identity, adopting many Ming cultural practices, while also employing local languages and cultural symbols to establish their legitimacy. In one illustrative example, the Qianlong Emperor (1736–96) had his face painted on the image of the Tibetan Buddhist Bodhisattva of Wisdom, Manjushri.

Rethinking the Westphalian miracle

As we saw above, institutionalists attach special significance to the 1648 Peace of Westphalia, arguing that by establishing a nascent system of sovereign states in Europe, it not only ended over a century of devastating religious conflict, it provided an enduring solution to the problem of cultural diversity. By making questions of culture, in the form of religion, an internal issue for sovereign states, it effectively secularized the international realm. And if this worked for religion, so it could (and would) for other issues of cultural difference: ethnicity, nationalism, civilization, etc. So long as states kept these to themselves, free to be whatever culturally they wanted within their borders, culture need never disrupt the wider peace. The list of scholars who celebrate this achievement is long indeed. Henry Kissinger, the realist former US Secretary of State mentioned earlier, writes that Westphalia 'shaped and prefigured the modern sensibility: it reserved judgement on the absolute in favour of the practical and ecumenical: it sought to distil order from multiplicity and restraint'. For the contemporary theorist of international relations Charles Kupchan, Westphalia 'would bring religious tolerance and political pluralism to Europe'. And John Ikenberry, who treats Westphalian sovereignty as the foundation of the 20th-century liberal international order, argues that the Peace established 'a relatively simple and durable principle of international order—that states that are recognized within this order have the right to choose their own form of government and religious orientation'.

The alternative perspective on culture and political authority sketched above casts serious doubt on these views about Westphalia and its legacy. Westphalia was not the pluralist moment that proponents claim. The treaties established a quintessential diversity regime, defining sovereign states as key centres of political authority, and authorizing only certain forms of cultural identity and expression as legitimate. Religion was the accepted axis of cultural difference, but only select Christian confessions were approved. Catholicism, Calvinism, and Lutheranism were sanctioned, but Judaism, Islam, and heretical Christian sects, like the Anabaptists, were unacceptable. Westphalia was thus a moment of great political-cultural engineering that created clear social hierarchies and patterns of inclusion and exclusion: any pluralism it established, was pluralism of the select.

Not only do proponents ignore all of this, they ignore the larger imperial context in which Westphalia took place. The emerging European system of sovereign states that Westphalia helped produce was nested within a network of overseas empires in Asia, the Americas, and the Atlantic. Here the prevailing diversity regime had a second, prior-existing, face. European empires were the legitimate forms of political authority, particularly in the Americas, and indigenous systems of political authority, from the Aztec, Inca, and Maya empires to the Indian nations of North America, were swept aside. All of this was justified on the basis of a clear cultural hierarchy, in which Christianity, inflected with white racism, warranted the subjugation and dispossession of non-European peoples.

Since the 17th century, the European, then global, international order has been structured by several diversity regimes, each of which has licensed a particular arrangement of political authority and tied this to accepted forms of cultural identification and expression. The regime instituted with the 1919 Peace of Versailles offers an interesting contrast to the Westphalian. After the wartime collapse of the Austro-Hungarian, German, and Ottoman empires, the victorious powers, led by US President Woodrow Wilson, sought to reorganize Europe on the principle of national self-determination, fundamentally reordering political authority on the continent. The polities granted sovereignty, however, were not principalities upholding favoured versions of the Christian faith, as they had been at Westphalia. They were select ethnically-defined nations: Czechs, Croats, Hungarians, Poles, Serbs, and others. Drawing clear territorial boundaries around such groups proved extremely difficult, though (e.g. with the breakdown of the Austro-Hungarian Empire, two-thirds of ethnic Hungarians lived outside the new state of Hungary). International laws thus had to be negotiated to protect ethnic minorities within the new nation-states (a move that proved tragically unsuccessful in stopping the widespread ethnic cleansing that followed).

Like the 17th-century diversity regime, the post-Versailles regime had an imperial face. The evolving system of sovereign states in Europe was the heartland of a far-flung system of empires. Wilson and his European counterparts were adamant that the principle of self-determination did not apply to the colonized peoples of Asia, Africa, and the Pacific. Beyond Europe, empire was to remain the legitimate form of political authority. Again, this political order was justified on cultural grounds. During the 19th century, the imperial powers had codified in international law a formal 'standard of civilization', distinguishing between civilized, barbarian, and savage peoples, and setting out the criteria on which they could be granted sovereign recognition. Europeans were deemed civilized, of course, and their sovereignty was never in question. Those defined as barbarians could rightly be subjected to European rule, but with proper guidance they were thought capable of both civilization and eventual independence. Savages, as most African and indigenous peoples were classified, were thought to be uncivilizable, and continued imperial rule was cast as essential.

This diversity regime—which combined sovereignty and ethno-nationalism in Europe, and empire and civilization abroad—collapsed after WWII. Its imperial face, however, remained largely intact. Although severely weakened by the war, European states clung tenaciously to their empires, often seeing their colonies as essential to post-war economic reconstruction. Some, like prominent historian Mark Mazower, argue that the UN was established, in part, as a way of preserving Western dominance and securing the imperial order. And in establishing the post-1945 'Trusteeship' system, which authorized Western rule of particular non-self-governing territories (such as the Belgian Congo, French Guiana, Indo-China, New Hebrides, Surinam, and South West Africa), the UN Charter defined such rule as a 'sacred trust'. The other face of the post-Versailles diversity regime fared far worse. The idea that peace in Europe could be secured by giving ethnically-defined nations self-determination was smashed by

Hitler's genocidal project of 'cleansing' the German nation and his aggressive campaign for a greater Germany. The international community emerged from the war allergic to ideas of ethnic nationalism, now favouring the civic ideal of nations of individuals united by their shared rights and responsibilities. As we saw in Chapter 6, this ideal found expression in the human rights principles enshrined in the core instruments of the international bill of rights. It was also an ideal that suited those struggling for independence in Europe's colonies. Empire remained a legitimate form of rule, and colonized peoples still had no right to self-determination. Yet the discrediting of ethnic nationalism suited anti-colonial activists, as most colonized peoples were culturally heterogeneous, defined as they were by territorial boundaries that were culturally arbitrary, the product of interimperial competition, economic opportunity, and geopolitical happenstance.

By 1970 the imperial face of this post-1945 diversity regime had disintegrated. We have already seen, in Chapter 6, how newly independent post-colonial states, working in the human rights forums of the UN, successfully redefined the right to self-determination as a prerequisite for the enjoyment of basic human rights and delegitimized the institution of empire. By the end of the 1960s empire had been defined as a crime, and civilizational hierarchy was no longer accepted as a valid justification for denying non-European peoples sovereign independence. A new diversity regime emerged at this point, one that continues today, albeit under highly contested conditions. For the first time in world history, this regime defines sovereign states as the primary, if not sole, legitimate centres of political authority. Pluralists might argue that even if Westphalia was not a pluralist moment, this was. But just as the Peaces of Westphalia and Versailles sought to shape the cultural profiles and practices of states, so too has the post-1970s regime. It establishes sovereign states as the dominant form of political authority, but the international community is not indifferent to the cultural practices of states.

The basic protections provided by the international bill of human rights have been augmented by a host of other treaties and conventions that limit acceptable cultural practices within states. The 1948 Genocide Convention, the 1992 UN Declaration on the Rights of Persons Belonging to National or Ethnic, Religious and Linguistic Minorities, the 1979 Convention on the Elimination of all Forms of Discrimination Against Women, the 2007 UN Declaration on the Rights of Indigenous Peoples, and the work of the United Nations Educational, Scientific, and Cultural Organization (UNESCO) all seek to constrain the exercise of sovereign power and shape the internal cultural practices of states.

This diversity regime is now under considerable challenge, as new configurations of global power and expressions of cultural difference intersect. Economic, military, and political power are rebalancing toward the East. New constellations of political power, evident in the rise of right-wing populism, are shaping the internal political terrain of many states, including the world's leading liberal democracies. And transnational actors, from multinational corporations to violent insurgents, are challenging sovereign states as the principal loci of political authority. All of this is entangled with the politics of culture, a notable feature of which is the return of cultural claims long thought (or hoped) extinct. Religion, ethno-nationalism, and civilization have all returned as the bases for claims on human identity and loyalty, and as moral bases on which to reorder prevailing arrangements of political authority. China's claims about the virtues of its Confucian civilization are designed not only to bolster internal political support for the Communist regime, but to push back against Western, liberal hegemony. Right-wing claims in Australia, Europe, and the US about the superiority of Western civilization are intended to do the opposite, to reassert Western hegemony. Ethno-nationalist movements across the world are seeking to roll back liberal legal and political institutions, and to resist the authority of international law and global organizations.

And transnational, religiously inspired insurgents are seeking to reshape the legal and political institutions of target states, combat Western, liberal cultural hegemony, and, as we saw in the case of ISIL, reshape an entire regional political order.

For culturalists, all of this spells the end of the modern international order, an order created by the West, for the West, and built upon, and sustained by, Western cultural values. Institutionalists, by contrast, hold strong in their faith that pluralist institutions, from Westphalian sovereignty to liberal multilateralism, will continue to contain the politics of culture. The alternative perspective developed above, however, poses the issue somewhat differently. Cultural diversity is nothing new to international relations: it has been a structural condition in which all of the most famous historical orders have evolved (recall the Ottoman and Qing), and has been there throughout the history of the post-Westphalian order. In all of these cases, institutions have been constructed to order cultural diversity, to delimit, channel, and harness it in ways conducive to particular forms of large-scale political rule. In the modern case, this has resulted in the construction of successive diversity regimes, the most recent of which combines universal sovereignty with international norms of human rights and multiculturalism. The key question, from this perspective, is whether this diversity regime has the adaptive capacities to accommodate today's new configurations of power and articulations of cultural difference, or whether we will see this disintegrate and the construction of a new global diversity regime.

Chapter 8
An essential political science

This little book makes a big claim. It argues that when seeking to understand international relations we should not limit our attention to external relations between sovereign states, as traditionally assumed, and we should not expand our gaze to the broader but amorphous realm of global politics, as some now propose. Rather, we should focus on the global organization of political authority, and on the human and environmental consequences of such organization. This retains the most valuable element of the traditional view, concentrating as it does on the nature and implications of one way of organizing political authority on a large scale: the system of sovereign states. The great limitation of such a view is its narrow focus, as if sovereignty was the only basis on which humans have ever organized authority. In reality, political authority has been configured in a variety of markedly different ways, most commonly into empires, complex heteronomous arrangements like feudal Europe, or some combination of these. Systems of sovereign states have been rare historically, and, as we have seen, today's global system is a very recent development.

Focusing on the global organization of political authority brings all of this into view, and in doing so provides a window on the shifting political conditions of human existence. As we have seen, the system of sovereign states and how states interact, both peacefully and violently, are no less important with such a focus. It enables us, however, to better understand the distinctiveness of this way of organizing politics, highlighting its unique institutional features (from sovereignty and international law to trade treaties and the International Bill of Rights), showing how it emerged historically, and enabling comparisons with other large-scale ways of arranging political authority (like the Ottoman and Chinese empires). More than this, we have seen that focusing on the global organization of political authority provides an illuminating framework for understanding issues that have long concerned students of international relations: the nature, effects, and control of war; the relationship between politics and economics; the significance of human rights; and the impact of cultural difference.

As we have seen, all of these are deeply connected with the definition, distribution, and institutionalization of political authority. War has helped create units of political authority (like sovereign states), served as a key marker of such authority, and been the object of authoritative control (through the laws of war, principally). The world economy, like all economies, depends on political authority to function. At the same time, however, the legitimacy of political authorities depends on the role they play in distributing economic goods, creating an imperative for them to manage not only their local economies but the broader regional or global economy as well. Struggles for individual and human rights have not been marginal to international relations, they have been a crucial engine for the reorganization of global political authority, contributing to the rise of today's global system of states and to the development of international norms limiting the scope of legitimate sovereign authority. Lastly, culture is neither the deep foundation of stable configurations of political authority (systems of states, empires, etc.) nor is it rendered politically irrelevant by supposedly pluralist institutions like sovereignty, multilateralism, or international law. Instead, all systems of political authority—local, regional, or global—emerge in culturally diverse environments, and the nature and organization of political authority has been deeply affected by the development of diversity regimes that relate legitimate political power to authorized forms of difference.

The advantages of focusing on the global organization of political authority go well beyond illuminating these key issues, however. Such a focus helps us better understand many of today's most pressing concerns as well. Indigenous peoples around the world are simultaneously struggling for recognition of their own social and political rights and challenging the legitimacy of settler colonial sovereignty. Struggles over the right to abortion, in the US and elsewhere, pit pro-life activists, who think that the authority of the state should extend to the control of women's bodies, against pro-choice campaigners, who reject such authority and insist on women's rights to control their own bodies. The authority of the International Criminal Court has been challenged by African states who claim that the Court has been biased in its prosecutions, targeting crimes in poor non-Western states while turning a blind eye to the aggression and war crimes of powerful Western states, like the US. The heated political debate in Britain about leaving the EU has ultimately concerned where political authority ought to lie, with 'Remainers' supporting continued membership and the authority of European institutions and 'Brexiteers' seeking to reassert their understanding of British sovereignty. The US withdrawal from key international treaties (like the Paris Climate Agreement), and its refusal to cooperate with leading international organizations (such as the WTO), have reflected the Trump Administration's robust belief that political authority should rest with the US, not international institutions. The escalating competition between China and the US is not just a struggle for economic or military supremacy: it is a struggle over political authority, over who has the right to define and uphold the rules of international relations, regionally and globally. These are but a few examples of how contests over the nature and location of political authority lie at the heart of contemporary international relations, and the list could go on and on.

Many worry that these current contests over the nature and location of political authority amount to a crisis in the modern international order. Central to this order has been US hegemony, but this is now waning and contested. Equally important has been international cooperation through multilateral institutions and organizations, such as the EU, the UN, and the WTO. But at the very time when humanity faces a myriad collective challenges—from combating new forms of organized violence and addressing growing economic inequality to dealing with the global climate emergency—such institutional cooperation appears to be flagging. Compounding all of this is the re-embrace of narrow conceptions of state sovereignty, reinforced by insular forms of populist nationalism. It is beyond the scope of this short book to assess, in any serious manner, the implications of these developments for the health or survival of the modern international order. But to the extent that this order has lain at the heart of the global organization of political authority since 1945 or earlier, the approach to international relations advanced in the preceding chapters would appear well-suited to comprehending such implications.

Let me end with a bold proposition about the place of international relations as an area of study within the broader discipline of political science. So long as international relations focused narrowly on external relations between sovereign states it could sit side-by-side with other sub-fields, like comparative politics, political theory, and studies of relevant national politics (American, Chinese, Indian, etc.). Indeed, other sub-fields could happily ignore international relations because it had focused itself on a separate domain of politics—the interstate. But when we reconceive international relations as centrally concerned with the global organization of political authority, such bracketing is no longer possible. In fact, international relations becomes an—if not the—essential political science. This doesn't mean that it fathoms all political processes and phenomena in all contexts, or that other sub-fields are redundant. Far from it. Rather, it means that international relations has a special—even indispensable—role addressing the macro-conditions—the global arrangements of legitimate political power—that condition politics in more local contexts, such as within sovereign states. My claim here is akin to that made by Immanuel Wallerstein (discussed in Chapter 5), who famously argued that sociologists should focus on the 'world social system', as the development of a single capitalist world economy had entwined all national social systems. My position is not quite so extreme or categorical, but my larger point is similar. In focusing on the global organization of political authority—whether that be today's system of states, the world of empires that preceded it, or some other large-scale configuration of legitimate political power—international relations addresses the overarching and encompassing political frameworks and processes in which local politics is inextricably entangled. This makes the study of international relations as vital as it is fascinating.

Glossary

African Union: A supranational organization of 55 member states, spanning the continent of Africa.

anarchy: A technical term used by international relations scholars when referring to a political system that lacks a central political authority, such as a system of sovereign states.

bilateralism: Cooperation between two states.

bipolar: Where power in an international system is dominated by two great powers.

Brexit: The term used to describe Britain's withdrawal from the European Union.

Constructivism: A theoretical perspective that emphasizes the socially constructed nature of international relations. In particular, how social norms and practices shape actors' identities, interests, and behaviour.

empire: A form of political organization in which a single imperial state exercises supreme authority over diverse peoples and polities. Such authority is usually formal, as in the Roman, Spanish, or British empires, but some hold that it can also be informal, citing the case of the US after 1945.

English School: A theoretical perspective on international relations which holds that, even in the absence of a world government, sovereign states can form international societies, animated by common interests, defined by shared rules, and upheld by international institutions.

epistemology: The study of, or ideas about, the nature and sources of knowledge.

European Union: A supranational organization of European states designed to promote political, economic, and cultural integration, and facilitate cooperation in the fields of security, economics, environment, and human rights.

Feminism: A theoretical perspective on politics and society, generally, and international relations, more specifically, that emphasizes the hierarchies of power, patterns of exploitation, and forms of violence produced by inequalities of sex and gender.

GDP (PPP): Gross Domestic Product calculated on the basis of Purchasing Power Parity. For an explanation, see https://ourworldindata.org/what-are-ppps

G20: The Group of Twenty. An international economic forum of 19 countries and the European Union.

G77: The world's largest international association of developing countries, with 134 members in 2019.

Global South: The preferred term used to describe low to middle income countries in Asia, Africa, Latin America, the Caribbean, and the Pacific.

hegemony: A form of political leadership, where a dominant state (the hegemon) is recognized by other states as having special rights and responsibilities in shaping international relations in collectively beneficial ways. The term is also used more broadly, to refer to the dominance of a set of ideas and practices: Western cultural hegemony, for example.

heteronomy: The principle that there exist simultaneously, in the same geographical space, multiple centres of authority (monarchies, empires, cities, religious institutions, etc.), and that these centres have overlapping, non-exclusive jurisdictions. Medieval Europe is the classic example of a heteronomous way of organizing political authority.

hierarchy: A socially accepted rank ordering of actors or institutions. Hegemony (defined above) is one example of hierarchy in international relations, another is the privileged role that great powers enjoy over other states.

institution: A set of formal or informal rules, norms, and practices that shape actors' identities, interests, and behaviour.

legitimacy: The quality of an actor, institution, or action that is considered good or rightful (e.g. the UN Security Council has legitimacy).

Liberalism: A general political theory that prioritizes the rights and interests of individuals, and, as a consequence, holds that the will of the people is the only true source of political authority. When applied to international relations, liberalism emphasizes the importance of democracy, multilateral cooperation, the rule of international law, human rights, and free trade.

multilateralism: Cooperation between three or more states based on reciprocally binding norms or rules.

multipolar: Where power in an international system is spread across a small group of great powers, commonly five to seven.

political authority: Political power that is considered legitimate.

power: The capacity to achieve a given set of ends, to shape the behaviour of others, to have transformative effects. Power is commonly seen as an attribute of certain actors, in certain social relationships. But it is widely accepted that social structures—like the unequal organization of an economy—can also have power, as can institutions, such as systems of law.

ontology: The study of, or ideas about, the nature of being. In particular, what comprises the natural and social worlds.

Postcolonialism: A theoretical perspective on international relations that emphasizes the political, economic, and cultural legacies of European imperialism, pointing in particular to an enduring global racial divide and to the inequalities produced by ongoing processes of racialization.

Realism: A theoretical perspective on international relations that emphasizes struggles for power between self-interested conflict groups, commonly sovereign states.

Renaissance: The period of European history between the fourteenth and seventeenth centuries, characterized by rapid and creative developments in the fields of culture, economics, politics, philosophy, and science.

Responsibility to Protect (R2P): The doctrine that state sovereignty is dependent on states honouring their responsibility to protect their populations, and that when states fail in this responsibility, the international community has a responsibility to provide such protection.

social contract: The idea that the authority of the state derives from the consent of individuals, and that under an imagined contract, individuals give up some of their natural freedoms and accept the authority of the state in return for the state protecting their new civil rights and maintaining social and political order.

sovereignty: The principle that the state is the supreme authority within its territory, and that it need recognize no higher authority beyond that territory.

state: A political and administrative institution. The most common kind of state referred to in international relations is the sovereign state, where the state enjoys exclusive political authority within specified territorial boundaries. Historically, however, there have been many other kinds of states, imperial states being the most common.

supranational: An institution or organization that has political or legal authority above and beyond that of sovereign states. Examples are the European Union and the United Nations.

suzerainty: A form of political authority in which one polity (often an empire) has authority over another polity (often termed a tributary), but where the latter retains significant independence, especially internally. The Chinese empire's relationship with states such as Japan, Korea, and Vietnam is often described as 'suzerain'.

transnational: Processes or phenomena that cross the territorial boundaries of sovereign states.

References

Chapter 1: What is international relations?

Raymond Aron, *Peace and War: A Theory of International Relations* (London: Weidenfeld and Nicolson, 1966), p.4.

Charles Dickens, *Hard Times* (Harmondsworth: Penguin Books, 1969), p.47.

Randolph Starn, *Ambrogio Lorenzetti: The Palazzo Pubblico, Siena* (New York: George Braziller, 1994), p.53.

Martin Wight, 'Why Is There No International Theory', in Herbert Butterfield and Martin Wight (eds), *Diplomatic Investigations: Essays in the Theory of International Relations* (London: George Allen and Unwin, 1966), p.26.

Chapter 2: The global organization of political authority

Jordan Branch, *The Cartographic State: Maps, Territory, and the Origins of Sovereignty* (Cambridge: Cambridge University Press, 2014).

Robert Gilpin, *War and Change in World Politics* (Cambridge: Cambridge University Press, 1981).

Edward Keene, *Beyond the Anarchical Society* (Cambridge: Cambridge University Press, 2002).

Christian Reus-Smit, *The Moral Purpose of the State* (Princeton: Princeton University Press, 1999), pp.12–13.

Christian Reus-Smit, *The Moral Purpose of the State* (Princeton: Princeton University Press, 1999), p.133.

John Gerard Ruggie, 'Multilateralism: The Anatomy of an Institution', *International Organization* 46:3 (1992), p.573.

John Gerard Ruggie, 'Territoriality and Beyond: Problematizing Modernity in International Relations', *International Organization* 47:1 (1993), pp.164–5.

Chapter 3: Theory is your friend

Alexander Anievas, Nivi Marchanda, and Robbie Shilliam (eds), *Race and Racism in International Relations* (London: Routledge, 2014).

Hedley Bull, *The Anarchical Society: A Study of Order in World Politics* (New York: Columbia University Press, 1977), p.13.

E. H. Carr, *What is History?* (Harmondsworth: Penguin, 1990), p.11.

Cynthia Enloe, *Bananas, Beaches, and Bases* (Berkeley, CA: University of California Press, 1990).

Cynthia Enloe, *The Big Push: Exposing and Challenging the Persistence of Patriarchy* (Berkeley, CA: University of California Press, 2018).

Martha Finnemore, *National Interests in International Society* (Ithaca, NY: Cornell University Press, 1996).

John Ikenberry, *Liberal Leviathan* (Princeton, NJ: Princeton University Press, 2011).

Robert Jackson, *The Global Covenant: Human Conduct in a World of States* (Oxford: Oxford University Press, 2000), p.420.

Immanuel Kant, *Perpetual Peace and Other Essays* (London: Hackett, 1983).

Robert Keohane, *International and State Power: Essays in International Theory* (Boulder, CO: Westview Press, 1989).

Audie Klotz, *Norms in International Relations* (Ithaca, NY: Cornell University Press, 1995).

Hans J. Morgenthau, *Politics among Nations* (New York: McGraw Hill, 1985).

Michael Oakeshott, *Experience and its Modes* (Cambridge: Cambridge University Press, 1933), p.99.

Christian Reus-Smit and Duncan Snidal, 'Between Utopianism and Realism: The Practical Discourses of International Relations', in Christian Reus-Smit and Duncan Snidal (eds), *The Oxford Handbook of International Relations* (Oxford: Oxford University Press, 2008), pp.3–40.

John Gerard Ruggie, 'Territoriality and Beyond: Problematizing Modernity in International Relations', *International Organization*, 47:1 (1993), pp.3–50.

Edward Said, *Culture and Imperialism* (New York: Alfred A. Knopf, 1993), p.19.

Laura Sjoberg, *Gendering Global Conflict* (New York: Columbia University Press, 2013).

Quentin Skinner, *Visions of Politics: Volume 1, Regarding Method* (Cambridge: Cambridge University Press, 2002), p.15.

J. Ann Ticker, *Gender in International Relations* (New York: Columbia University Press, 1992).

Jacqui True, *The Political Economy of Violence against Women* (Oxford: Oxford University Press, 2012).

Kenneth Waltz, *Theory of International Politics* (New York: Random House, 1979).

Alexander Wendt, *Social Theory of International Politics* (Cambridge: Cambridge University Press, 1999).

Chapter 4: War

Hedley Bull, *The Anarchical Society* (New York: Columbia University Press, 1977), p.185.

The Charter of the United Nations, 26 June 1945. https://www.un.org/en/sections/un-charter/un-charter-full-text/

The Covenant of the League of Nations, 28 June 1919. http://avalon.law.yale.edu/20th_century/leagcov.asp

Lawrence Freedman, *The Future of War: A History* (Penguin: Harmondsworth, 2017), p.x.

General Act of the Berlin Conference on West Africa, 26 February 1885. https://www.sahistory.org.za/archive/general-act-berlin-conference-west-africa-26-february-1885

Institute for Economics and Peace, Global Terrorism Index 2018: Measuring the Impact of Terrorism. http://visionofhumanity.org/app/uploads/2018/12/Global-Terrorism-Index-2018-1.pdf

The Kellogg–Briand Pact, 27 August 1928. http://avalon.law.yale.edu/20th_century/kbpact.asp

Royal Charter to Sir Walter Raleigh 1584. http://avalon.law.yale.edu/16th_century/raleigh.asp

Thucydides, *History of the Peloponnesian War* (Harmondsworth: Penguin, 1972), pp. 401–2, 536–7.

Max Weber, 'Politics as a Vocation', in H. H. Gerth and C. Wright Mills, *Max Weber* (New York: Oxford University Press, 1970), p.78.

Chapter 5: Economy

Eric Helleiner, *Forgotten Foundations of Bretton Woods: International Development and the Making of the Postwar Order* (Ithaca, NY: Cornell University Press, 2016).

Vladimir Lenin, *Imperialism: The Highest Stage of Capitalism* (Harmondsworth: Penguin, 2010).

McKinsey Global Institute, *Digital Globalization: The New Era of Global Flows*, March 2016. https://www.mckinsey.com/~/media/McKinsey/Business%20Functions/McKinsey%20Digital/Our%20Insights/Digital%20globalization%20The%20new%20era%20of%20global%20flows/MGI-Digital-globalization-Full-report.ashx

OECD (Organization for Economic Co-operation and Development), *Economic Outlook*, No.89 (May 2011), pp.290–1.

Esteban Ortiz-Ospina, Diana Beltekian, and Max Roser, 'Trade and Globalization', *Our World in Data*, October 2018. https://ourworldindata.org/trade-and-globalization

Reserve Bank of Australia, 'The International Trade in Services', *Bulletin* (March 2019). https://www.rba.gov.au/publications/bulletin/2019/mar/the-international-trade-in-services.html

Jeremy Rifkin, 'The 2016 World Economic Forum Misfires with its Fourth Industrial Revolution', *Huffpost*, 14 January 2016. https://www.huffpost.com/entry/the-2016-world-economic-f_b_8975326

Klaus Schwab, 'The Fourth Industrial Revolution: What it Means, and How to Respond', *World Economic Forum: Global Agenda*, 14 January 2016. https://www.weforum.org/agenda/2016/01/the-fourth-industrial-revolution-what-it-means-and-how-to-respond/

These GDP figures are calculated by Purchasing Power Parity (PPP). A graphic illustration of changes in national GDP since 1800 can be found at: https://www.youtube.com/watch?v=4-2nqd6-ZXg

United Nations Conference on Trade and Development (UNCTAD), 'South-South Integration is Key to Rebalancing the Global Economy', *UNCTAD POLICY BRIEFS*, No.22, February 2011.

Immanuel Wallerstein, *The Capitalist World Economy* (Cambridge: Cambridge University Press, 1979).

World Inequality Lab, *World Inequality Report 2018*, p.11. https://wir2018.wid.world/files/download/wir2018-full-report-english.pdf

WTO (World Trade Organization), *World Trade Report 2013: Factors Shaping the Future of World Trade* (Geneva: WTO Publications,

2013), p.54 (cited twice). https://www.wto.org/english/res_e/
booksp_e/world_trade_report13_e.pdf

Chapter 6: Rights

Alexander Betts and Phil Orchard (eds), *Implementation and World
Politics: How International Norms Change Practice* (Oxford:
Oxford University Press, 2014), p.2.

Ronald Dworkin, *Taking Rights Seriously* (Cambridge, MA: Harvard
University Press, 1978), p.365.

Joel Feinberg, *Rights, Justice, and the Bounds of Liberty* (Princeton,
NJ: Princeton University Press, 1980), p.151.

Margaret Keck and Kathryn Sikkink, *Activists beyond Borders* (Ithaca,
NY: Cornell University Press, 1998).

Audie Klotz, *Norms in International Relations: The Struggle against
Apartheid* (Ithaca, NY: Cornell University Press, 1995).

John Locke, *Two Treatises of Government* (Cambridge: Cambridge
University Press, 1988), p.279.

Samuel Moyn, *The Last Utopia: Human Rights in History*
(Cambridge, MA: Harvard University Press, 2010). For extended
critiques of Moyn's argument, see Christian Reus-Smit, *Individual
Rights and the Making of the International System* (Cambridge:
Cambridge University Press, 2013); and Kathryn Sikkink, *Evidence
for Hope: Making Human Rights Work in the 20th Century*
(Princeton, NJ: Princeton University Press, 2017).

Christian Reus-Smit, *Individual Rights and the Making of the
International System* (Cambridge: Cambridge University Press,
2013).

Christian Reus-Smit, *Individual Rights and the Making of the
International System* (Cambridge: Cambridge University Press,
2013), p.154.

Thomas Risse, Stephen C. Ropp, and Kathryn Sikkink (eds), *The
Power of Human Rights: International Norms and Domestic
Change* (Cambridge: Cambridge University Press, 1999).

Thomase Risse, Stephen C. Ropp, and Kathryn Sikkink (eds), *The
Persistent Power of Human Rights* (Cambridge: Cambridge
University Press, 2013).

United Nations, *Universal Declaration of Human Rights*. http://www.
un.org/en/udhrbook/pdf/udhr_booklet_en_web.pdf

Chapter 7: Culture

Karen Barkey, *Empire of Difference: The Ottomans in Comparative Perspective* (Cambridge: Cambridge University Press, 2008), p.8.

Pamela Kyle Crossley, *A Translucent Mirror: History and Identity in Qing Imperial Ideology* (Berkeley: University of California Press, 1999), p.31.

Terry Eagleton, *Culture* (New Haven, CT: Yale University Press, 2016), p.1.

G. John Ikenberry, 'Liberal Internationalism and Cultural Diversity', in Andrew Phillips and Christian Reus-Smit (eds), *Culture and Order in World Politics* (Cambridge: Cambridge University Press, 2019), p.146.

Image of Qianlong Emperor as Manjushri, Buddhist Bodhisattva of Wisdom. https://www.freersackler.si.edu/object/F2000.4/

Robert Jackson, *The Global Covenant* (Oxford: Oxford University Press, 2000), pp.112, 106.

Henry Kissinger, *World Order: Reflections on the Character of Nations and the Course of History* (London: Allen Lane, 2014), p.8.

Charles A. Kupchan, *No One's World: The West, The Rising Rest, and the Coming Global Turn* (Oxford: Oxford University Press, 2012), p.32.

Mark Mazower, *No Enchanted Palace: The End of Empire and the Ideological Origins of the United Nations* (Princeton, NJ: Princeton University Press, 2009).

President Barack Obama, 'President Obama's UN Speech: Defending World Order', 24 September 2014. https://obamawhitehouse. archives.gov/the-press-office/2014/09/24/remarks-president-obama-address-united-nations-general-assembly (accessed 29 December 2017).

Christian Reus-Smit, *On Cultural Diversity: International Theory in a World of Difference* (Cambridge: Cambridge University Press, 2018); and Andrew Phillips and Christian Reus-Smit (eds), *Culture and Order in World Politics* (Cambridge: Cambridge University Press, 2019).

Amartya Sen, *Identity and Violence: The Illusion of Destiny* (Harmondsworth: Penguin, 2006), pp.xii–xiii.

Ann Swidler, 'Culture in Action: Symbols and Strategies', *American Sociological Review*, 5:2 (1986), 273–86.

President Donald J. Trump, 'Remarks by President Trump to the People of Poland, July 6, 2017', p.12. https://www.whitehouse.gov/

the-press-office/2017/07/06/remarks-president-trump-people-poland-july-6-2017 (accessed 11 December 2017).

Martin Wight, *Systems of States* (Leicester: University of Leicester Press, 1977), pp.33, 238.

Raymond Williams, *Keywords: A Vocabulary of Culture and Society* (London: Fourth Estate, 2014), p.84.

Ayse Zarakol, 'The Ottomans and Diversity', in Andrew Phillips and Christian Reus-Smit (eds), *Culture and Order in World Politics* (Cambridge: Cambridge University Press, 2019), Chapter 3.

Further reading

Chapter 1: What is international relations?

John Baylis, Steve Smith, and Patricia Owens (eds), *The Globalization of World Politics* (Oxford: Oxford University Press, 2020 Eighth Edition).

Michael Zurn, *A Theory of Global Governance* (Oxford: Oxford University Press, 2018).

Chapter 2: The global organization of political authority

Jane Burbank and Frederick Cooper, *Empires in World History* (Princeton, NJ: Princeton University Press, 2010).

Barry Buzan and George Lawson, *The Global Transformation: History, Modernity, and the Making of International Relations* (Cambridge: Cambridge University Press, 2015).

Jean L. Cohen, *Globalization and Sovereignty: Rethinking Legality, Legitimacy, and Constitutionalism* (Cambridge: Cambridge University Press, 2012).

Tim Dunne and Christian Reus-Smit (eds), *The Globalization of International Society* (Oxford: Oxford University Press, 2017).

Ayse Zarakol, *After Defeat: How the East Learned to Live with the West* (Cambridge: Cambridge University Press, 2011).

Chapter 3: Theory is your friend

Geeta Chowdhry and Sheila Nair, 'Introduction: Power in a Postcolonial World: Race, Gender, and Class in International Relations', in Geeta Chowdhry and Sheila Nair (eds), *Power, Postcolonialism and International Relations* (London: Routledge, 2002).

Michael Doyle, *Ways of War and Peace: Realism, Liberalism, and Socialism* (New York: Norton, 1997).

Martha Finnemore, *National Interests in International Society* (Ithaca, NY: Cornell University Press, 1996).

Jennifer Sterling Folker, *Realism and Global Governance* (London: Taylor and Francis, 2019).

Beate Jahn, *Liberal Internationalism: Theory, History, Practice* (London: Palgrave, 2013).

Cornelia Navari and Daniel Green (eds), *Guide to the English School in International Studies* (Chichester: John Wiley & Sons, 2014).

Sanjay Seth (ed.), *Postcolonial Theory and International Relations* (London: Routledge, 2013).

Jacqui True, *The Political Economy of Violence Against Women* (Oxford: Oxford University Press, 2012).

Chapter 4: War

Severine Autesserre, *The Trouble with the Congo: Local Violence and the Failure of International Peacebuilding* (Cambridge: Cambridge University Press, 2010).

Janina Dill, *Legitimate Targets: Social Construction, International Law, and US Bombing* (Cambridge: Cambridge University Press, 2014).

Beatrice Heuser, *The Evolution of Strategy: Thinking War from Antiquity to the Present* (Cambridge: Cambridge University Press, 2010).

Isabel V. Hull, *A Scrap of Paper: Breaking and Making International Law during the Great War* (Ithaca, NY: Cornell University Press, 2014).

Hew Strachan and Sibylle Scheipers (eds), *The Changing Character of War* (Oxford: Oxford University Press, 2011).

Chapter 5: Economy

For the old view of European take-off, see Douglass C. North and Robert P. Thomas, *The Rise of the Western World* (Cambridge: Cambridge University Press, 1973), and for the argument about globalization from Asia and the Middle East, see John M. Hobson, *The Eastern Origins of Western Civilization* (Cambridge: Cambridge University Press, 2004).

Jacqueline Best, *Governing Failure: Provisional Expertise and the Transformation of Global Development Finance* (Cambridge: Cambridge University Press, 2014).

Patricia Clavin, *Securing the World Economy: The Reinvention of the League of Nations, 1920–1946* (Oxford: Oxford University Press, 2016).

Penny Griffin, *Gendering the World Bank: Neoliberalism and the Gendered Foundations of Global Governance* (London: Palgrave, 2009).

Branko Milanovic, *Global Inequality: A New Approach for the Age of Globalization* (Cambridge, MA: Belknap Press, 2016).

Adam Tooze, *Crashed: How a Decade of Financial Crises Changed the World* (Harmondsworth: Penguin, 2019).

Chapter 6: Rights

Mary Ann Glendon, *A World Made New: Eleanor Roosevelt and the Universal Declaration of Human Rights* (New York: Random House, 2001).

Stephen Hopgood, Jack Snyder, and Leslie Vinjamuri (eds), *Human Rights Futures* (Cambridge: Cambridge University Press, 2017).

Lynn Hunt, *Inventing Human Rights* (New York: Norton, 2008).

Margaret Keck and Kathryn Sikkink, *Activists beyond Borders* (Ithaca, NY: Cornell University Press, 1998).

Beth Simmons, *Mobilizing for Human Rights: International Law and Domestic Politics* (Cambridge, MA: Harvard University Press, 2009).

Julia Suarez-Krabbe, *Race, Rights and Rebels: Alternatives to Human Rights and Development from the Global South* (Lanham: Rowman and Littlefield, 2015).

Chapter 7: Culture

Amitav Acharya, *Civilizations in Embrace: The Spread of Ideas and the Transformation of Power; India and Southeast Asia in the Classical Age* (Singapore: Institute for Southeast Asian Studies, 2012).

Alexander Anievas, Nivi Manchanda, and Robbie Shilliam (eds), *Race and Racism in International Relations* (London: Routledge, 2014).

Peter J. Katzenstein (ed.), *Civilizations in World Politics* (New York: Routledge, 2009).

Andrew Phillips and Christian Reus-Smit (eds), *Culture and Order in World Politics* (Cambridge: Cambridge University Press, 2020).
Elizabeth Shakman Hurd, *Beyond Religious Freedom: The New Global Politics of Religion* (Princeton, NJ: Princeton University Press, 2015).

Index

For the benefit of digital users, indexed terms that span two pages (e.g., 52–53) may, on occasion, appear on only one of those pages.

A

activists, human rights 95–7, 99–100
agricultural trade 69–71
Algeria 57–8
Allegory of Good Government (Lorenzetti) 3–4, 43–4
anarchical society 41, 45–6
Ancient Greece 15–16
Anievas, Alexander 44–5
ANZUS (Australia, New Zealand, US) Treaty 14
apartheid 95–7
arbitration 60–2
Aron, Raymond 2–3
assumptions 32–5 *see also* theoretical approaches
Australia
Austro-Hungarian Empire 114

B

Barkey, Karen 111
basic institutional practices 15–16

Berlin Conference on West Africa (1884–5) 20–2, 59–60
Betts, Alexander 97–9
bipolar distribution of power 25–6
'Boomerang' pattern of transnational infuence 95–7
Branch, Jordan 17
Bretton Woods system 75–8
Brexit 11–14, 19–20, 121–2
Bull, Hedley 41, 47, 49, 54–5

C

capitalism 65, 67–8, 71–2
Carr, E. H. 32–3
cartography 17–25
Catalan map of the Mediterranean 22–4
CEDAW *see* Convention on the Elimination of Discrimination Against Women
Charles V, Holy Roman Emperor 89
children, individual rights 93–4

China 117–18
  conflict with US 121–2
  economy 73, 79
  Qing Empire 112
  South China Sea 11–14
Chinese suzerain order 5
climate change 81
Cold War 78–9
command economies 78–9
communism 79
Constitution of Cadiz (1812) 90–1
constitutional institutions 16
constitutional norms 25–6
constructivism 39–41
contracts 85–6
Convention against Torture and
    Other Cruel, Inhumane
    or Degrading Treatment
    (CAT) 93–4
Convention on the Elimination
    of Discrimination Against
    Women (CEDAW) 14–15,
    93–4
Convention on the Prevention and
    Punishment of the Crime of
    Genocide (CPPCG) 93–4
Convention on the Rights of the
    Child (CRC) 93–4
covenants, on individual rights 93–5
criminal court, international 60–2
Crossley, Pamela Kyle 112
cultural diversity 109–12, 118
culturalist view 102–3, 105–9, 118
culture 9, 102
  definition 103–5

D

decolonization 74–6
  post-1945 87–8, 91–4, 105–6,
    115–17
deindustrialization 69–70
democracy 37–8
Dickens, Charles 8
digital revolution 70–2

diplomacy 14–16
discrimination, laws against 93–4
diversity regimes 109–11, 115–18
Dworkin, Ronald 87

E

Eagleton, Terry 103–4
East India Company 56–7
Eight Banners system 112
Elizabeth I, Queen of England 56–7
empires
  collapse of 87–8, 90–2
  cultural diversity 111–12
  hierarchies 88–9
  map of world's empires (1900)
    20–2
  political authority 5–7, 12
  post-colonialism 44–6
  shift to sovereign states 25–8,
    74–6
  and war 56–8
English School 41–2, 105–6
Enloe, Cynthia 43–4
environmental crisis 81
ethnic cleansing 100, 110
Europe
  collapse of empires 28
  contemporary political map
    17–20
  decolonization 74–5
  industrial revolution 69–70
European Convention on Human
    Rights (ECHR) 94–5
European Union, Britain's
    withdrawal from 11–14, 19–20,
    121–2
exchange rates 76–7

F

Feinberg, Joel 87
feminism 43–4
financial crises 64, 68–9, 75–6, 80
Finnemore, Martha 40–1

Ford, Henry 71–2
free trade 37–8, 76–7
Freedman, Lawrence 50
fundamental institutions 15–16

G

Gandhi, Mahatma 69–70
gender equality 93–4, 99–100
General Agreement on Tariffs and
    Trade (GATT [later
    WTO]) 14, 76–8
general rights 85–9
Geneva Conventions 57–8, 60
genocide 60–2, 100, 110
    laws against 93–4
Gilpin, Robert 25–6
Global Financial Crisis (2008) 64,
    68–9, 75–6, 80
global politics 2
Global South 73
globalization 69–71, 73
Group of Twenty (G20) 81–2
Gulf War (1990–1) 54–5

H

Hague Convention (1899) 20–2, 60
Hague Convention (1906) 20–2
hegemony 26, 36–9, 73, 75–6
Helsinki Accords (1975) 19–20
heteronomous political
    authority 22–5
hierarchies 45–6
Hitler, Adolf 115–16
Holy Roman Empire 89–90
human rights 86–7
    international norms 40–1
    see also individual rights
humanitarian interventions 59–60

I

ICC see International Criminal
    Court

ICCPR see International Covenant
    on Civil and Political Rights
identity 39–40
    cultural 105, 109
Ikenberry, John 38–9, 106–7,
    112–13
IMF see International Monetary
    Fund
India
    British Empire 56–7
    individual rights covenants 93
individual rights 9, 83
industrial revolutions 69–72
inequality, economic 81
institutionalist view 102–3, 105–9,
    112–13, 118
institutions 13–17
    constitutional 16
    fundamental 15–16
    issue-specific 14–16, 27
    managing global economy 76–7
    money as 67–8
    vs. organizations 14
    protection of individual
        rights 92–7
    US withdrawal from 121–2
    and war 54–5
International Bill of Rights 93–4
International Covenant on Civil
    and Political Rights
    (ICCPR) 14–15, 93–4
International Covenant on
    Economic, Social and
    Cultural Rights (ICESCR) 93
International Criminal Court
    (ICC) 60–2, 94–5, 121–2
International Criminal Tribunal
    for Rwanda 94–5
International Criminal Tribunal
    for the Former Yugoslavia
    94–5
international law 37–9
International Monetary Fund
    (IMF) 76–7, 79
international norms 40–1

international organizations, political authority 5–6
international regimes *see* issue-specific institutions
international relations, definition 1–3
International Whaling Association 11–12
interventions 59–60
Iraq, Gulf War (1990–1) 54–5
Islamic State of Iraq and the Levant (ISIL) 11–12
issue-specific institutions 14–16, 27
Italy 56–7

J

Jackson, Robert 45–6, 106–7
Japan 5
   departure from the International Whaling Association 11–12

K

Kant, Immanuel 37–8
Keck, Margaret 95–7
Keene, Edward 20
Kellogg–Briand Pact (1928) 59–60
Keohane, Robert 38–9
Kissinger, Henry 105–6, 112–13
Klotz, Audie 40–1, 95–7
Korea 5
Kupchan, Charles 112–13

L

Latin American independence 87–8, 90–1
League of Nations 20–2, 53–4, 60–2
Lenin, Vladimir 67–8
LGBTQI rights 99–100
liberalism 37–9, 106–7
Lifanyuan system 112
Locke, John 87
Lorenzetti, Ambrogio 3–4, 43–4

M

Manchanda, Nivi 44–5
manufacturing trade 69–71
Mao Zedong 79
maps 17–25
market competition 67–8
market economies 78–9
material power, vs. institutional politics 13–14
materialism 36–7
   and war 47
Mazower, Mark 115–16
Mediterranean, map 22–4
mercenaries 57–8
military power 36
money as a social institution 67–8
monopolies 67–8
morality, and individual rights 87
Morgenthau, Hans 36
Moyn, Samuel 100–1
multilateralism 15–16
multipolar distribution of power 25–6

N

Napoleon Bonaparte 90
nationalism 117–18, 122
Native American tribes 5
New International Economic Order (NIEO) 74–5
new orders 53–4
Nixon, President Richard 77
non-territorial challenges 27
Nuclear Non-Proliferation Treaty (NPT) 14–15

O

Oakeshott, Michael 32–3
Obama, President Barack 107–8
Orchard, Phil 97–9

Organization for Economic
      Co-operation and Development
      (OECD) 70–1
organizations, vs. institutions 14
organized violence, war as 49–51,
      62–3
Ottawa Convention on
      Anti-Personnel
      Landmines 14–15
Ottoman Empire 68–9, 111

P

Paris Climate Agreement 11–12
peace conferences, following
      war 53–4
Peace of Augsburg (1555) 89
Peace of Westphalia (1648) 87–90,
      106–7, 112–18
planned economies 78–9
pluralism 41–2, 116–17
political authority 3–5, 120–2
   and economies 67–9
   empires 20–2
   and gender 43–4
   and global economy shifts 74–82
   and individual rights 84–7
   maps 17–25
   Middle Ages 22–5
   organization of 5–7, 11–13, 17–27,
      38–42
   realist viewpoint 36–7
   and war 48–58
political hegemony 26, 36–9,
      75–6
populism 68–9, 117–18, 122
Portolan chart 22–4
post-colonialism 44–6
power
   and gender 43–4
   struggle for 36
   theories about 33
power distribution 25–6
property rights 40–1

Q

Qing Chinese Empire 112

R

R2P see Responsibility to Protect
racial inequality 44–6
Raleigh, Sir Walter 56–7
realism 36–7
Reformation 89, 106–7
Renaissance 17
Responsibility to Protect (R2P)
      41–2, 54–5, 59–60, 100
Rifkin, Jeremy 72
rights 9, 83
right-wing populism 117–18, 122
Risse, Thomas 97–9
Rome Statute of the International
      Criminal Court 14–15
Ropp, Stephen 97–9
Ruggie, John 14, 27, 40–1
Russia, gender inequality 11–12,
      99–100

S

Said, Edward 44–5
Schwab, Klaus 72
Scramble for Africa 20–2, 59–60
self-determination, right to 91–2,
      115–16
Sen, Amartya 105
Sepoy Rebellion (1857–8) 56–7
shared rules 41–2
Shilliam, Robbie 44–5
Sikkink, Kathryn 95–9
Sjoberg, Laura 43–4
Skinner, Quentin 32–3
social structures 39–40
solidarism 41–2
South Africa, apartheid 95–7
South China Sea 11–14
sovereign rights 84–5

sovereign states 2, 119–20
  created after war 53–4
  cultural organization 110, 116–18
  empire-building 20–2
  exclusive property rights 40–1
  formation 87–8
  institutional politics 13–14, 16
  legitimate use of violence 55–8
  mapping 17–20
  political authority 3–6, 12
  protection of individual
    rights 92–3, 95, 97–9
  recognition of rights 42
  shared rules 41–2
  transformation to 25–8, 74–6
  war between 49
sovereign-imperial system 27–8
Soviet Union 79
Spanish Empire 90–1
special rights 85–6
spiral model of human rights
    change 97–9
state boundaries 17–20, 24–5
superpowers 25–6
supranational bodies, political
    authority 5–6
Swidler, Ann 105
systemic change 25–7
systems change 25–8

T

technological revolutions 71–2
terrorism 50–1, 57–8, 62–3
theoretical approaches 8, 29
Thucydides 47–8
Tickner, Ann 43–4
Tilly, Charles 52
torture, laws against 93–4
trade, global 69–71
transformation, from empires to
    sovereign states 25–8, 74–6
transnational actors, political
    authority 5–6

transnational advocacy
    networks 95–7, 100
Trans-Pacific Partnership 13–14, 78
treaties 14–15
Treaty of Versailles (1919) 53–4, 114
True, Jacquie 43–4
Trump, President Donald 107–8

U

unipolar distribution of power 25–6
United Kingdom (Great Britain)
  Brexit 11–14, 19–20, 121–2
  economy 73
  political hegemony 26
  'special relationship' with US 14
United Nations (UN) 20–2
  Charter (1945) 14, 16, 27–8,
    59–62, 91, 115–16
  Framework Convention on
    Climate Change
    (UNFCCC) 14–15
  High Commissioner for Refugees
    (UNHCR) 5–6
  human rights tribunals 94–5
  Security Council 54–5, 59–62
United States (America)
  attitudes towards Canada and
    Cuba 39–40
  conflict with China 121–2
  distribution of power 25–6
  economy 73, 77
  hegemony 26, 75–6
  'special relationship' with UK 14
  withdrawal from international
    institutions 11–12, 121–2
Universal Declaration of Human
    Rights (1948) 93–4

V

Vietnam 5
violence
  legal restrictions 58

legitimate use by sovereign
    states 55–8
organized 49–51, 62–3

W

Wallerstein, Immanuel 65, 122–3
Waltz, Kenneth 36
war 8, 47
    arbitration 60–2
    legal combatants 57–8
    legal restrictions 58–62
    and male dominance 43
    as organized violence 49–51, 62–3
    types of weapons 60
war crimes 60–2
wars of constitution 50–1, 62–3
wars of position 50–2, 62–3

Wars of Religion 89
wars of state-making 50–2, 62–3
Weber, Max 48, 55–6
Wendt, Alexander 39
Wight, Martin 5–6, 105–6
Williams, Raymond 103–4
Wilson, President Woodrow 114–15
women's rights 93–4, 99–100
World Bank 79
World Trade Organization (WTO
    [formerly GATT]) 14, 76–8
World War II
    institutions formed after 14–15
    principle of sovereignty 19–20

Z

Zarakol, Ayse 111

THE UNITED NATIONS
A Very Short Introduction
Jussi M. Hanhimäki

With this much-needed introduction to the UN, Jussi Hanhimäki engages the current debate over the organization's effectiveness as he provides a clear understanding of how it was originally conceived, how it has come to its present form, and how it must confront new challenges in a rapidly changing world. After a brief history of the United Nations and its predecessor, the League of Nations, the author examines the UN's successes and failures as a guardian of international peace and security, as a promoter of human rights, as a protector of international law, and as an engineer of socio-economic development.

www.oup.com/vsi

THE U.S CONGRESS
A Very Short Introduction
Donald Richie

The world's most powerful national legislature, the U. S. Congress, remains hazy as an institution. This *Very Short Introduction* to Congress highlights the rules, precedents, and practices of the Senate and House of Representatives, and offers glimpses into their committees and floor proceedings to reveal the complex processes by which they enact legislation. In *The U.S. Congress*, Donald A. Ritchie, a congressional historian for more than thirty years, takes readers on a fascinating, behind-the-scenes tour of Capitol Hill-pointing out the key players, explaining their behaviour, and translating parliamentary language into plain English.

www.oup.com/vsi

THE SOVIET UNION
A Very Short Introduction
Stephen Lovell

Almost twenty years after the Soviet Unions' end, what are we to make of its existence? Was it a heroic experiment, an unmitigated disaster, or a viable if flawed response to the modern world? Taking a fresh approach to the study of the Soviet Union, this Very Short Introduction blends political history with an investigation into the society and culture at the time. Stephen Lovell examines aspects of patriotism, political violence, poverty, and ideology; and provides answers to some of the big questions about the Soviet experience.

www.oup.com/vsi

THE EUROPEAN UNION

A Very Short Introduction

John Pinder & Simon Usherwood

This *Very Short Introduction* explains the European Union in plain English. Fully updated for 2007 to include controversial and current topics such as the Euro currency, the EU's enlargement, and its role in ongoing world affairs, this accessible guide shows how and why the EU has developed from 1950 to the present. Covering a range of topics from the Union's early history and the ongoing interplay between 'eurosceptics' and federalists, to the single market, agriculture, and the environment, the authors examine the successes and failures of the EU, and explain the choices that lie ahead in the 21st century.

www.oup.com/vsi

INTERNATIONAL MIGRATION
A Very Short Introduction
Khalid Koser

Why has international migration become an issue of such intense public and political concern? How closely linked are migrants with terrorist organizations? What factors lie behind the dramatic increase in the number of women migrating? This *Very Short Introduction* examines the phenomenon of international human migration - both legal and illegal. Taking a global look at politics, economics, and globalization, the author presents the human side of topics such as asylum and refugees, human trafficking, migrant smuggling, development, and the international labour force.

www.oup.com/vsi